The Slow Food Story

The Slow Food Story

Politics and Pleasure

GEOFF ANDREWS

McGill-Queen's University Press

MONTREAL & KINGSTON • ITHACA

ISBN   978–0–7735–3477–3 (cloth)
ISBN   978–0–7735–3478–0 (paper)

Legal deposit third quarter 2008
Bibliothèque nationale du Québec

Published simultaneously outside North America by Pluto Books

Library and Archives Canada Cataloguing in Publication

Andrews, Geoff, 1961–
    The slow food story : politics and pleasure / by Geoff Andrews.

Includes bibliographical references and index.
ISBN 978–0–7735–3477–3 (bound).—ISBN 978–0–7735–3478–0 (pbk.)

    1. Slow food movement. 2. Slow food movement—History. 3. Food.
4. Gastronomy. 5. Environmental responsibility. I. Title.

HD9000.5.P27 2008   641.3   C2008–902126–6

Designed and produced for the publisher by
Chase Publishing Services Ltd, Sidmouth, EX10 9QG, England
Typeset from disk by Stanford DTP Services, England
Printed and bound in the United States of America

Contents

Preface

I first encountered the Slow Food movement in July 2001. In Genoa for the G8 summit, on one of the first peaceful demonstrations before the violence which was to characterise those days, I came across a banner displaying the words 'Lucca Slow Food'. There were many different peace and political groups at Genoa, including many from Tuscan towns like Lucca, which marked the beginning of a new phase of associationism, and I did not pay it much attention at the time. Later however, when I was travelling in Italy writing about the new associations and thinking about cultural politics in Italy, the fate of the Italian Left, and an alternative future for the beautiful and complex country to the one provided by Silvio Berlusconi's populism, I returned to Slow Food. I visited Bra, the small town of 20,000 people in Piedmont which is the home of the movement, interviewed Carlo Petrini and wrote a chapter for my book *Not a Normal Country*.

This was not enough however. The movement was growing and clearly held a significance well beyond Italy. The first Terra Madre was held in late 2004 which opened up Slow Food to producers from all over the world. It was now a significant political movement addressing a range of concerns, including those of 'critical consumers' in the West, poor producers in the South of the world, the contradictions between obesity and famine and the costs and consequences of globalisation. One of the remarkable things about Slow Food, it seemed to me, was the way in which it could appeal to different types of people in very different circumstances. This suggested it was a movement with a real presence and purchase on the popular political imagination. It seemed to have the ear of restaurateurs, farmers and policy makers, while retaining a radical and principled position sufficient to capture the imagination of anti-global activists and environmentalists.

If Slow Food's ideological provenance was the Italian Left, it had extended well beyond the conventional language of the militant activist and addressed a multitude of worries about food. In Britain and the US, for example, the relentless drive of 'fast life', whether through the dominance of fast food outlets or supermarkets, was reshaping not only diets but civic and cultural life. There were few spheres that escaped the pervasive influence of the dominant corporate values which amounted to the imposition of a particular way of living. The New Labour government in Britain seemed to epitomise this celebration of corporate culture, managerialism and the so-called knowledge economy. Its higher education strategy, whereby students were to be put on a university production line for future employment, now involved McDonald's in management training initiatives. Even my own institution, the Open University, founded in the late 1960s as a modern and progressive institution, entered into an extraordinary deal with Tesco in 2007, whereby students would get their tuition fees reduced according to how much they spent at Britain's largest retail outlet.

The phrase 'Slow Food', which would appear increasingly in restaurant reviews, newspaper articles about farmers' markets, and TV programmes about the quality of life, would come to be used as a counter to these trends – an offer of something different, which questioned the pace of modern life while restating the importance of aesthetic pleasure. To some, Slow Food was a nostalgic retreat from the realities of the contemporary world, offering at best a temporary respite for those who could afford the luxury of eating local produce. However, as I got to know the movement better, it became apparent that in its defence of the simple pleasures of food it offered a complex and prescient response to life in the era of globalisation.

My first visit to the US opened my eyes to another world than that which I had understood as the 'fast food nation'. In 2005, I travelled to some unlikely Slow Food destinations, including the hills of Wisconsin and the centre of Cleveland, Ohio. From my interviews here and in Chicago, New York, and later San Francisco, it was evident that we were seeing the beginnings of an alternative food network with varied roots ranging from Henry D. Thoreau's call to 'simplify, simplify' ways of living, working and eating, during his time at Walden Pond near Concord, Massachusetts in the 1850s, to the counter-culture in Berkeley, California in the 1960s.

In the UK, Slow Food was mainly a rural movement driven by concerned citizens, forgotten farmers and self-taught gastronomes, though its influence was growing in the metropolis and in the outlook of food critics, writers and chefs. In countries outside Italy, food and related issues were now at the top of many political agendas, with politicians seeking solutions for obesity and other health concerns, worries over the quality of life of new generations, the impact of supermarkets and environmental crises. It became apparent, however, that Slow Food would not succeed as a modern political movement, and would be far less interesting as a topic of research, if it did not also engage with the global struggles around food.

As I discovered, the new politics of food was attracting greater attention from academics, with the arrival of new food studies departments, courses on gastronomy, and demands for changes in educational curricula to meet the new and challenging questions. Thankfully these concerns over food have not been left to politicians and experts but have been taken up by the new gastronomes, whether public figures like the British TV chef Jamie Oliver, or the growing number of critical consumers and activists.

Yet Slow Food remains an Italian-directed association, and the cultural and regional context in which food cultures thrive there has continued to shape the movement. Part of

Slow Food's appeal lies in the admiration many hold for the sheer capacity for 'good living' that is indicative of Italy, its economic problems and political inertia notwithstanding. The book starts here, therefore. An intriguing local story that has become a global phenomenon.

Acknowledgements

I have received enormous help from Slow Food members and organisers from several different countries, whether through formal interviews, email correspondence or informal chats over dinner. All interviews which appear as unattributed quotes in the text were carried out by myself. In the Slow Food offices in Bra, I would like to thank Paola Nano, Elisa Virgillito and Francesca Rosso in the Press Office for responding to my numerous queries; Lilia Smelkova for her Eastern European contacts and insight into the development of Slow Food in these countries; Giada Talpo, Julia Vistunova, Alberto Arosso (also for finding me an apartment), Olivia Reviglio, Paola Gho, Carmen Wallace, Cinzia Scaffidi, Giulio Colomba, Anya Fernald (and later after she moved back to San Francisco), Silvia Monasterolo, Alessandro Monchiero, Alberto Farinasso, Sibilla Gelpke and Elena Aniere. I am grateful to Alberto Capatti and Nicola Perullo at the University of Gastronomic Sciences, and to one of their brightest students, Allison Radecki, for lots of ideas and insight.

In Sicily I received enormous help from Rosario Gugliotta, who met me at Milazzo as I embarked from Salina and drove me to the Nebrodi mountains to meet producers of the 'suino nero', and then back to Messina province to meet Attilio Interdonato, the latest in a long line of noted lemon producers. Aldo Bacciulli gave me a tour of Catania fish market and produced an astonishing meal at Metro, his restaurant in the centre of town. I don't know what I would do in Sicily without Natalie Guziuk, who has now driven me around her adopted island and arranged dinners and meetings in the cause of two of my books. She also introduced me to Gianni Samperi, who not only makes the best honey in Sicily, but is a very convivial host.

I am very grateful to my friend Hugh Tisdale who, in 2005, drove me 2,468 miles in nine days across the US – a 'fast' introduction to the fascinating slow movement in the US. His tolerance of my erratic navigating and his insight into the ideas of Thoreau were also much appreciated. In the New York office of Slow Food I am grateful to Erika Lesser and Deena Goldman for answering many queries and Ed Yowell, New York Convivium leader, for taking me round the Greenmarket in Union Square. In San Francisco I would like to thank Slow Food co-leaders Carmen Tedesco and Lorenzo Scarpone for showing me around; Michael Dimock for his insight on the development of Slow Food; and Eleanor Bertino, who took me to a fine Italian restaurant and shared her memories of her time with Alice Waters in the 1960s. In Chicago I am grateful to Joel Smith for showing me around his city, including the unique city farm. In Cleveland, Ohio, Kari Moore showed us the city and took us to lunch at Sokolowski's; Linda and Fred Griffin provided excellent hospitality and enabled me to meet other members of the Cleveland convivium over dinner. In Wisconsin I am grateful to Deb Deacon, John and Dorothy Priske and Erika Janik for a very pleasant and enlightening afternoon.

Jacek Szklarek was a great host in Poland, driving me from Warsaw to Krakow and introducing me to producers and chefs. While in Poland I attended a Slow Food Foundation–Fair Trade conference and benefited from meeting Laura Gandolfi and other colleagues from CEFA and Fair Trade Italia. I am grateful to Jim Turnbull of Adept for putting me in touch with colleagues working on the ground in Romania: Ben Mehudin, Anca Calagar and Charles; the last two drove me around some beautiful and remote parts of Transylvania and introduced me to the jam producers of the region. One of these, Gerda Gherghiceanu, also provided excellent hospitality in the Saxon village of Viscri. Cristi Gherghiceanu and Raul Cazan discussed the origins of Slow Food in Romania with me and shared their recollections of the revolution of 1989 during an excellent evening in Bucharest.

I first met Fiona Richmond, formerly the UK's Slow Food co-ordinator, in Bra, and she has subsequently been a great source of contacts and enthusiasm as my book developed. Thanks also to those in the British Slow Food delegation to the Mexico Congress who were good company, and to Katy Davidson, Silvija Davidson, David Natt, John and Rosemary Fleming, Nick Howell, David and Sue Chantler, Donald Reid, Wendy Fogarty, Peter and Juliet Kindersley, John Kenward, Sue Miller, Susan Flack in Aylsham and other members of the British Slow Food movement who have helped me in various ways.

In Berlin I am very grateful to Otto Geisel, Ulrich Rosenbaum and Thomas Struck for stimulating insight into the German Slow Food movement. In Norway, the Oslo convivium leader, Marit Mogstad, was very helpful and hospitable, and Ove Fossa told me about the Norwegian Presidia products during lunch at Terra Madre. In Zurich my friend Stefan Howald gave me a history of the Swiss radical tradition; I am also grateful to Marc Aerni and Rainer Riedi.

Many other people have helped me in various ways with their insight and suggestions, and I am grateful to the following: Zeenat Anjari, John Dickie, Samuel Muhunyu, Roberta Sassatelli, Emanuele Di Caro, Michael Gleeson, Filippo Ricci, Matteo Patrono, Clive Barnett, Luigi Coldagelli, Lele Capurso, Stefano Sardo, Hugh Mackay, Matt Staples, Professor Engin Isin and the Centre for Citizenship, Identity and Governance at the Open University, Federica Davolio, Gordon Smith, Reparata Mazzola, and Gordon Jenkins for arranging the interview with Alice Waters. My co-editors at *Soundings* have sustained my political appetite over recent years and my first articles on Italy and Slow Food appeared there. I am grateful to David Hayes, my editor at *Open Democracy*, who has been a great source of encouragement for my writing for a long time now.

Finally, I would like to thank friends in Bra, intermittently my home since 2005. Nicola Ferrero, John Irving, Giovanni Ruffa, Paola Nano, and Marcello Marengo have provided conviviality and encouragement on many occasions. I am grateful to John Irving for information, suggestions and new contacts. Many long lunches with John in Badellino's have ended with new ideas, as we attempted to set the world of food (and football) to rights under the attentive, if somewhat bemused, eyes of our hosts, Giacomo and Marilena. Badellino's is one of many excellent convivial restaurants I have enjoyed in the course of my research and I have provided a list of some of the others at the end of the book.

Geoff Andrews

Part One

Ideas

1
Politics in Search of Pleasure

IN RAUCOUS SCENES in the Senate, Italy's upper house of parliament, an opposition member of Silvio Berlusconi's Forza Italia party is stuffing himself with *mortadella*, the spicy, fatty sausage from Bologna. Another colleague bursts open a bottle of champagne. 'Please, gentlemen', pleaded Franco Marini, the speaker of the Senate, as he attempts to restore order. 'This is not an osteria'.

The occasion is the defeat of Romano Prodi's government in January 2008 and the allusion is to Prodi's nickname, '*mortadella*', derived from his affinity to his home city and his 'cheeky chops'. The scene is indicative of the kind of spectacle that has come to characterise what passes for politics in modern Italy. In fact, the defeat of this government threw Italy into its worst crisis since the *Tangentopoli* ('Bribesville') scandal of the early 1990s when the Christian Democrats, who had governed Italy for most of the post-war years, virtually collapsed overnight.

It confirmed moreover that Italy had once again shown itself incapable of reform and that the gap between its political class and its citizens had reached unprecedented and dangerous levels. In the weeks leading up to the government's defeat, a rubbish dispute in Naples had left the city paralysed, with dangerous litter and waste strewn over the streets, the citizens in uproar at the incompetence and corruption of its rulers (the camorra – the local mafia – had control of refuse contracts), and Italy's

EU allies looking on with bemusement. In Sicily during the same period, the island's governor, Salvatore 'Toto' Cuffaro, had been found guilty of 'helping the mafia', was sentenced to five years imprisonment and banned from public office. 'I'll be at my desk as usual tomorrow', an exultant Cuffaro announced, as if he had been exonerated, and mindful that the length of the appeals process will make it unlikely he will go to prison. No wonder. Italy's political leaders, according to Sergio Rizzo and Gian Antonio Stella, are a 'caste', untouchable, too easily given to corruption and contemptuous of their critics.[1] It is not without irony that one of the outspoken critics of a farcical political system should be the blogger Beppe Grillo, one of the country's best loved comedians.

These events in 2008 proved that the 'clean hands' investigations led by the magistrate Antonio Di Pietro in the 1990s, and the anti-mafia reforms of the same period, had not succeeded. The historical context, always important in Italian political identity, was evident again with the biggest divisions between left and right seen in Italy since the fascist years. The main beneficiary of the long-term crisis in Italian politics was Silvio Berlusconi, Italy's richest man, whose populism since the mid 1990s turned Italy into the most degenerate body politic in Western Europe, raising fears and uncertainty not seen since the 1970s. In that period, Italy was a country in turmoil, with the *anni di piombo*, the 'years of lead', reflected in the terrorist violence of right and left which questioned the legitimacy of the state.

Yet the 1970s, where this story begins, was also a time of great idealism and creativity, when young people were being drawn to movements rather than parties, and culture increasingly became a site of political protest. In the wake of the events of 1968 in Paris, and the 'hot autumn' of student unrest and workers' struggles in Italy in 1969, many on the Italian Left had sought different political avenues, including the *Il Manifesto* group which split from the Italian Communist Party and set up the newspaper of the same name. As the 1970s got underway, social movements started to challenge the hegemony of political parties, their more autonomous grassroots structures and more direct forms of action inspiring a new generation of young people. It is in this cultural and political moment that we find the origins of Slow Food, one of the most significant global political movements of modern times. A group of young left-wing activists, including Carlo Petrini, Azio Citi and Giovanni Ravinale, from the small Piedmont town of Bra, near the hills of the Langhe, renowned for its Barolo, Barbera and Dolcetto red wines, as well as its white truffles, shared similar ideals to the radical generation. In 1974 they launched a monthly left-wing newspaper *In Campo Rosso* (In Red Domain), which ran until 1985. More ambitious initiatives followed.

On 17 June 1975, in a building on Piazza XX Settembre, in the centre of Bra, Italy's first independent political radio station transmitted its first programme. *Radio Bra Onde Rosse* (Radio Bra Red Waves) was launched from the top of what is now the Hotel Giardini. The group wanted to change the world, and broadcasting on 'red waves' would be the way to reach their fellow citizens. They needed a bigger space for their ideas and in order to counter the mainstream news coverage emanating from Bra's only newspaper. As a pirate radio station with communist affiliations (they refused to accept advertising), Radio Bra was a very controversial experiment in Italy; within a month of opening it was closed down by the police, who confiscated equipment. After a wide public campaign which brought Dario Fo and Roberto Benigni to the town in support of a huge protest, Radio Bra was back on air, helped ultimately due to a constitutional court ruling which led to a liberalisation of radio laws in Italy (the same laws, ironically, which allowed Silvio Berlusconi's rise as a media entrepreneur a decade later). In addition to Radio Bra, the trio maintained their growing public voice and kept their politics local; in 1975 they opened both a bookstore, the *Cooperativa Libraria La*

Torre (Tower Book Co-op) in nearby Alba, and a grocery store selling local products, the *Spaccio di unità popolare* (or Store of Popular Unity).[2]

The group had also joined the PDUP (the Democratic Party of Proletarian Unity), an 'extra-parliamentary' Marxist group which had become disillusioned with the strategy of Italy's main communist party (PCI), the largest in Western Europe, at the time locked into a 'historic compromise' with the Christian Democrats. In 1975 they even managed to get one of their number, Carlo Petrini, elected to the Bra town council, which helped raise their profile further. Petrini was the only member of the council opposed to the historic compromise, but council representation was not enough to satisfy the aspirations of the Bra radicals, who wanted to change the world.

The politics of Petrini and his friends remained rooted in cultural modes of expression, with a very strong regional identity. In 1978, the trio participated in the Club Tenco – a group of socialist musicians whose president was the singer Paolo Conte – at Italy's well-known popular music festival of San Remo. They performed as a group, nicknamed the 'short, the tall and the fat', and produced a cabaret of songs and jokes. In 1979 they held the first *Cantè i'euv* international festival. This was derived from a Piedmontese folk music tradition which involved visiting farmhouses in the Langhe at night and literally 'singing for eggs'. Traditionally those who took part included a small band playing violin, trombone and accordion. The farmers, including those who were awoken from their beds, invariably came out, provided something to eat, danced and joined in the fun. The *Cantè i'euv* was a tradition that was dying out, and Petrini and his friends helped to revive it.[3]

The participants at the *Cantè i'euv* festival included international musicians from Russia, Sweden, Ireland, Britain and France, and the involvement of the Piedmont region in the organisation and funding of the event (which ran for three years) was a sign of things to come in the later organisational structure of Slow Food (as was the attempt to rescue important local traditions – in this case folk music – at risk of extinction). More important was the celebration of music for its sheer enjoyment and pleasure. Stefano Sardo, the son of Piero Sardo, one of the *Cante' i'euv* organisers, remembers from his childhood the exciting atmosphere, and casual drug use, of the Russian pianist and other musicians who stayed overnight at his house. They were carefree idealists. These were the early signs of the politics of pleasure which was to shape the origin and development of Slow Food.

Petrini and his comrades from Bra, who called themselves the 'philoridiculous' group, were also members of Arci, the cultural and recreational federation of the Italian Left, which had been formed in 1957. Arci had different sections on football, trekking and film amongst other things, and its Langhe federation became increasingly focused on local culture, driven by a growing desire to reconnect with the traditions of the area. Initially, Petrini was stirred by the need to preserve and develop local wine. There was concern that Piedmont had declined as a wine-producing region and the wine producers in Barolo and other areas were facing big difficulties in producing and selling wine. These concerns were aired in regular discussions at the home of one of the Barolo producers, Bartolo Mascarello, who was a left sympathiser and regularly hosted intellectuals, journalists and left-wing political figures at his *cantina*. In October 1981, Petrini and some of his friends founded the 'Free and Meritorious Association of the Friends of Barolo', in the Castello dei Falletti, a castle in Barolo.[4] The slogan of the association was '*Barolo è democratico, o quanto meno puo diventarlo*' ('Barolo is democratic or at least it can become so').[5]

In 1982, Petrini and a group of fellow Arci Langhe members set off to visit Montalcino in Tuscany to celebrate the *Sagra del Tordo*, the festival of the thrush. Taking lunch in the local *Casa del Popolo*, the workers' social club, Petrini and his friends were horrified by the meal they were served: the pasta was cold, the salad was dirty, and it was declared inedible. On their return to Bra, Petrini wrote a strong letter of complaint to the *Casa del Popolo* and the secretary of the Tuscany Arci group. He argued that the meal was 'not worthy of the most beautiful *Casa del Popolo* and the place which produces the most prestigious wine'. This provoked a stiff response from Andrea Rabissi, President of the local Arci branch, who accused Petrini of 'ugly' and 'senseless' allegations. He replied that there were more important things that deserved the attention of the left than eating in a certain style.

In the ensuing debate in the pages of *L'Unità*, the newspaper of the PCI, and in a public meeting the following April which centred on the relationship between the *Case del Popolo* and the gastronomic tradition, views became polarised between eating well – in this context, the symbol of pleasure – and the left's immediate political priorities. It became a debate over the nature of politics itself. The *Casa del Popolo* in Montalcino, according to the town's then communist mayor, Mario Bindi, was in 'turmoil' and the local branch of Arci was divided. There was, however, one long-term benefit of Petrini's intervention for Montalcino: in later years the town held a gastronomic fair at the *Casa del Popolo* as well as competitions between restaurants of communist branches. It seemed that he had won over some of the party faithful.

The divisions at the *Casa del Popolo* mirrored a wider crisis on the left at this time. Petrini later recalled that the PCI's attitude towards pleasure and good food was to treat it as one of the 'seven capitalist sins'. The parliamentary left was focused on day-to-day battles and electioneering, and constrained by the entrenched nature of Italy's *partitocrazia*, the post-war state run by the dominant political parties in their own interests. Its view of politics was narrowing. On the other hand, the new generation of activists in the social movements took a more expansive view of politics. 'The personal is political' was one of the themes of the 1960s and 1970s, and the 'personal' was bound up with questions of freedom, leisure, artistic appreciation and quality of life. The quality of cultural life, including access to, and appreciation of, food and wine, was a democratic question. The pursuit of pleasure was everybody's concern, and was not to be left to hedonists and elitists.

An important step had been taken in the development of gastronomic associations on the left. Indeed this shift now started to resonate with other developments outside the Langhe. The osteria movement is an important example. Left activists started to open co-operatives, osterias and trattorias, the traditional eating establishments of ordinary people. In the Langhe, the *Cooperative I Tarocchi* provided the framework for the birth of new osterias and brought together left-wing wine enthusiasts including Gigi Piumatti, Firmino Buttignol and Marcello Marengo, who would begin a long association with Slow Food. This movement went beyond the Langhe however. Near the Arci offices in the centre of Rome, activists had long been meeting in a wine bar in Via Cavour, a milieu which included not only Petrini, but Valentino Parlato of *Il Manifesto* and Massimo Cacciari, a philosophy professor and later Mayor of Venice. In this bar Petrini introduced his comrades in Arci and *Il Manifesto* to the neglected wines of Piedmont. The osteria movement in Bra included the setting up of the *Osteria Boccondivino*, opened in 1984 in Via Mendicita Istruita 12, an address it was later to share with the Slow Food office, with Carlo Petrini amongst the waiters for the inaugural dinner.

The year 1986 was a key moment in the development of Slow Food. The formation of *Arci Gola* ('gola' meaning appetite) in Barolo in July, with Petrini unanimously elected as its first President, was the culmination of the critical dialogue within the Italian Left at this time. *Arci Gola* (later Arcigola) was supported by *Il Manifesto* and other left papers and grew to be one of the biggest sections in Arci. In many ways this marked the formation of Slow Food with an organisational structure evolving across the regions of Italy. In December *Il Manifesto* published the first issue of *Gambero Rosso* (Red Prawn) as a wine supplement. *Gambero Rosso* was to grow into one of Italy's leading wine guides, accompanying Slow Food's own *Osterie d'Italia* guide. Indeed Arcigola's main partners at this time were wine producers.

The most renowned Italian wines of the period were mainly from Chianti and elsewhere. Piedmont wine was still recovering from its lost years. Another event in the Piedmont region in 1986 was to prove a watershed in the development of Slow Food for quite different reasons. In the Langhe 19 people died from contaminated wine, after cheap wine produced in the small town of Narzole had been spiked with methanol to increase the alcohol content. The tragedy had a devastating effect on the reputation of Piedmontese wine and was regarded as a serious betrayal of consumers (1986, of course, was also the year of the Chernobyl disaster and the fears of pollution and contamination were felt at a more global level). In the face of this tragedy, wine consumption dipped by half and there was a real need to recover the reputation of local wine as well as the trust of consumers. The recognition of quality became a major concern for Arcigola activists, alongside their wider goal of educating people about the pleasures of wine.

The 1980s saw a departure from the idealism of the previous two decades. Italy was being shaped by a moment of economic and social change, and unashamed individualism, described by some as 'Milano da bere', 'the Milan you can drink'. This was the equivalent of Thatcherism in the UK, or Reaganomics in the US, and was associated in Italy with the rise of Silvio Berlusconi, who accumulated most of his media industries during this period, and began his long ascent to power with glossy TV programmes and the first reality shows. It was characterised by the value of superficiality, of getting rich quick, and the celebration of wealth. Pleasure itself was reduced to superficiality to many critics. According to Cinzia Scaffidi – now head of Slow Food's study centre and who first became involved in politics at this time – this was a new 'individualism' which 'opened many dangerous doors'. The superficiality of the period extended to food, with the first fast food stores arriving in Italy and the rejection of traditional recipes and food knowledge.

A demonstration organised by Arcigola in 1986, outside the intended site of a McDonald's near the Spanish Steps in the centre of Rome (the second to arrive in Italy), was a response to these developments and marked a more public demonstration of Arcigola's politics. Following this demonstration, the term 'Slow Food' was first used and a manifesto was produced which would take the ideas of the association beyond Italy. The poet and writer Folco Portinari was given the task of writing the Slow Food Manifesto. In preparing the new movement's philosophy Portinari has acknowledged a variety of influences, from the speed-inspired manifesto of Marinetti's Futurists in 1909 to the 'Fellows Feeding Machine' in Charlie Chaplin's *Modern Times*. His Manifesto challenged the ethical basis of what he called 'fast life' and was critical of those 'who can't tell the difference between efficiency and frenzy'. In condemning the ways in which the 'virus of fast life' had imposed its false set of values, Portinari celebrated the virtues of Slow Food, based on sensual pleasures and wisdom. The Slow Food Manifesto, according to Petrini and Portinari, was initially a defensive strategy, in response to the pervasiveness of the fast life virus, but its alternative emphasis on pleasure both resonated with the earlier political backgrounds of many of the signatories, while also articulating an alternative way of living. The Slow Food Manifesto was first published in *Il Manifesto* on 3 November 1987 in the *Gambero Rosso* supplement, and was also published in *La Gola* magazine the same month. Petrini and Portinari headed a list of left-wing signatories.

It was the publication of the Slow Food Manifesto which exported Slow Food's idea beyond Italy and set in motion the beginnings of a remarkable 'movement', as people started to refer to it; the English wording undoubtedly helped to 'globalise' and publicise its appeal to all those who had concerns about the spiralling of fast food. Following the publication of the Manifesto in several different languages and in a shortened version, Petrini and his comrades issued international press releases and set a date for a launch of Slow Food as an international movement in Paris in December 1989. This ceremony, attended by 250 Slow Food delegates from Italy who ate a meal cooked by a combination of Italian and French chefs, attracted wide press coverage. It marked the beginning of a movement which now has 84,000 members in over 120 countries, an international office staff in Bra of around 150, and which organises a series of international events. If its origins lay in the political leanings of a small group from Bra, its scope was global and would present a political challenge not only to the way food was produced and consumed but the values of the society underpinning it.

The 1960s and 1970s were the pivotal decades which shaped the politics of the Slow Food movement in Italy. They were also influential in shaping the direction of Slow Food USA, which has become the second largest Slow Food association. When Patrick Martins set up the Slow Food office in New York in March 2000 – following a couple of years working in the Bra office – there were only 212 members and 5 convivia. However, he and his successor Erika Lesser have drawn on a rich and radical legacy emanating from the counter-cultural movements of the 1960s. It was in Berkeley, California, in the midst of student protests, that Alice Waters – founder of Chez Panisse restaurant and later Slow Food's International Vice-President and the unofficial ambassador of Slow Food USA – received her political apprenticeship. In 1964, at the height of the protests at Berkeley, and not long after the assassination of John F.

Kennedy, Waters had transferred from Santa Barbara (where she expected to get married and raise a family from her early twenties). At Berkeley she joined the Free Speech Movement and met many of the activists who were involved in the various campaigns for civil rights, against the Vietnam war and in favour of sexual liberation. The attempts of the university authorities to prevent political activity on the campus met with furious resistance that would merge into major social and cultural movements over the following years, in parallel to those in France, Italy and Western Europe. One of the leaders of the Free Speech Movement was Mario Savio, an effective orator from a Sicilian background, who led an occupation of the main university offices in December 1964. This led to a violent response from the police. Waters got to know Savio, and she was impressed not only by his oratory but also by the bottles of wine on his table, and his ability to talk of 'physics and poetry'. His effect on her, she told me, was similar to the impact Carlo Petrini would have years later.

For Waters, the counter-culture she encountered at Berkeley changed her life forever. 'We had the sense that we could do anything and we could change the world. We wanted to live differently.' This feeling was soon transferred to food, and she has said that it was the new freedoms driven by the Berkeley counter-culture which gave her the confidence to open a restaurant, to do things differently, and to reach out to like-minded people. The trigger for this interest in food was her first visit to France in 1965, where she was inspired by the French approach to cooking, using ingredients from the local market. 'I saw how food was part of everybody's life, rich or poor, intellectual or not. People were sitting down to dinner. They shopped at local shops.'

After graduating, and spending a year in London learning the Montessori method, Waters started teaching, an event which influenced her later dedication to the power of education to change lives through the school gardens projects, as well as

influencing the philosophy behind her restaurant, notably
the commitment to 'direct sensory experience, experimenta-
tion, optimism, confidence'.[6] She had already formed ideas
about starting a restaurant; partly inspired by dinner parties
she hosted for a new circle of film directors, actors and
intellectuals. French movies were intensely popular amongst
the young Berkeley radicals, with Waters particularly taken
with the films of Marcel Pagnol.

Waters' passion for food was now part of the intellectual
discussions of this circle and her dream of opening a restaurant
was getting closer. With the support of some friends, and
'hippy' carpenters, Waters bought a run-down house in
Berkeley and opened the Chez Panisse restaurant in August
1971, the name inspired by a character in a Pagnol movie.
Her targeted clientele from the early days were professors and
students, to whom she offered special set menus; however,
from the very beginning Waters did not compromise on quality
ingredients. According to friends and colleagues at the time,
she was an idealist and a 'spendthrift' who had little inclination
to worry too much about budgeting. Waiters and waitresses
were usually artistic types, including film or drama students,
poets and potters.[7]

From the outset then, pleasure was central to Waters' idea
of changing food culture in the US. This was reflected not
only in the food but also in the culture which surrounded
the employees of Chez Panisse, with Led Zeppelin and David
Bowie playing in the restaurant's kitchen, and marijuana,
cocaine and drink not uncommon amongst the waiters. Though
the menus gradually got more sophisticated, notably in the
years in which Jeremiah Tower was head chef (1973–75), the
'simple' message sent out by Waters was groundbreaking in
understanding future global questions concerning such issues
as sustainability, the organic movement and healthy food. This
message was clear: use simple, fresh ingredients, be uncom-

promising on quality and promote the convivial atmosphere of a neighbourhood restaurant.[8]

The counter-culture was crucial to the development of the movement in the US, and has remained a theme in the development of Slow Food, reflected in the idea of 'Slow Food Nation' – the name of US Slow Food's biggest event to date, in San Francisco in late August 2008. Alice Waters herself is convinced of the continued relevance of the counter-culture in the contemporary era of globalisation. Her sixties' idealism continues to drive her politics. 'I want to green the United Nations. I want gardens on the White House lawn. I want a peace garden in the Gaza Strip.'[9]

The food writer Michael Pollan also believes the 1960s were formative in the development of the Slow Food movement in the US. He points to several continuities, including the 'back to the land movement', the hippy communes, Woodstock and the Diggers, which all had strong roots in rediscovering rural ways of living and 'building a new society', even though people did not use the term 'organic' with any great conviction. The strongest link with the earlier era was the groundbreaking idea that 'the personal is political'. This found many expressions in sexual politics and the civil rights movement but was also fundamental to the way in which food has become a political issue. According to Pollan, food has become one of the ways in which people make personal political choices. He told me that the 'personal' dimension to food is 'what people are responding to today', whether as activists in alternative consumption movements or just acting as informed citizens, they are making personal choices about the food they eat which often go against received opinion or the power of big corporations. The contemporary politics of food thus has deep roots in the counter-culture, and Pollan himself is based in California, the centre of the sixties' movements, which remains the heartbeat of Slow Food USA, with a strong intellectual milieu, a sophisticated food culture and some of the most active Slow Food convivia (the name of Slow Food's local branches).[10]

There are crucial similarities too between Waters and Petrini (who first met in California in the early 1990s). Both have been described as visionaries of their movements, even utopians who want to change the world through cultural politics. Both are perfectionists in their commitment to the quality of food, which partly seems to reflect unshakeable principles developed in their early years of activism, principles which have not been significantly compromised even though both have had to be pragmatic in pursuing their various projects and schemes. Both have had disastrous experiences with money: in Waters' case, this was in the early years of Chez Panisse, when the restaurant almost went out of business; in Petrini's it was the loss of funds in one of his early projects. For both, money was secondary to their wider purpose and rarely got in the way of their latest ideas. Indeed both draw sharply on the sixties' principles of thinking the unthinkable and demanding the impossible. 'It is not the first time we have had a crazy idea', Petrini would say to colleagues asked to deliver his latest scheme. '"Of course it's possible", Ms Waters would often say when someone told her that something could not possibly work.'[11] In their expanding circles they have both proved very adept at influencing people who matter.

Yet, we have to ask how this Italian-style association, inspired by the movements of the 1960s and 1970s, could appeal to a wider constituency of more than 84,000 members in over 120 countries? More intriguingly, how did this movement, which originated on the periphery of the Italian Left, begin to root itself in countries with such different histories, traditions and political cultures as the US, Germany, post-communist Romania, Mexico and the United Kingdom? How did it appeal to such different types of people as metropolitan intellectuals, peasant farmers, restaurateurs, urban employees, anti-globalisation activists and rural workers, drawing in at the same time, as John Dickie has put it, 'hedonistic first-world consumers and hard-pressed third-world producers'?[12]

The answer to this can be found in the uneven world of globalisation where food has risen to the top of the political agenda in a less rigid ideological age and where new and more autonomous political subjects have challenged the authority of experts through a re-articulation of traditional knowledge. Slow Food's critique is aimed essentially in the direction of contemporary global capitalism and its varying impact on the quality of life. It presents a critical engagement with contemporary lifestyles: representing not a simple contrast between 'tradition' and 'modern', but a response to contemporary ways of living, whereby concerns around food are rooted in wider issues over the effects of globalisation, the disparity between obesity and famine, environmental crisis, the impoverishment of small farmers, and increasing global economic inequality.

It reflects a desire on the part of quite different people for an alternative way of living, in which pleasure is central, whether as an ideal to be reclaimed from industrialised and standardised rituals of Anglo-American capitalism, or from the bland, routinised legacy of Eastern European communism, or as a necessary condition of survival from corporate multi-nationals in developing countries. This idea of pleasure is reflected in many different cultural and national expressions in the contemporary global world, but was evident from an early stage in the intellectual origins of Slow Food.

Slow Food's philosophy appeals to members in different countries, with different political histories and traditions. Indeed, as it has grown in Italy and the US, it has found resonance in some less likely places, relatively untouched by the political legacy of the 1960s and 1970s, for example in the hills of Wisconsin, or remote parts of southern Italy. At its simplest, this philosophy is one which seeks to defend the traditional pleasures of food under threat from the standardisation of produce and fast food. Yet it does have a sophisticated body of ideas. Its core ideological principle, which has organised its agenda since the mid 1990s, is 'eco-gastronomy'. The combination of a concern for the environment with the pleasures associated with the production, preparation, cooking and consumption of food is Slow Food's most distinctive feature. It has become the main intellectual focus for framing its political agenda and has provided a new source of political identity for its members.

The emphasis on gastronomy is partly derived from the ideas of Jean-Anthelme Brillat-Savarin who, in *Physiologie du goût* (The Physiology of Taste), saw gastronomy as encompassing 'analytical knowledge of everything related to man's eating'.[13] This holistic approach which incorporates the work and interests of farmers, winegrowers and chefs, as well as bringing together pleasure and good health, has been adopted by Slow Food with a modern interpretation. In France in the late eighteenth and early nineteenth century it was associated with the new sophistication of the post-revolutionary bourgeoisie, giving birth to a new gastronomic literature and helping good food and restaurants to gain cultural prominence among the emerging elite.

Slow Food's modern interpretation of gastronomy is grounded in the costs and consequences of the modern diet, the world of globalisation and the new interest in food culture. Gastronomy is no longer the preserve of the elite, nor can it be reduced to the popular TV food expert, who offers little cultural analysis or knowledge of the history of food. Gastronomy, to Carlo Petrini, is an interdisciplinary science which cuts across the traditional spheres of intellectual enquiry. He quotes Brillat-Savarin approvingly and with an eye to the contemporary world. Gastronomy 'is the reasoned knowledge of everything concerning man in so far as he eats ... It is gastronomy that moves the growers, the wine-makers, the fishermen and the numerous family of cooks.'[14] Gastronomy, according to Petrini, should now be at the centre of the network of connections between producers, consumers and public debates about food: it is at the interchange of local and global places and cultures. Yet, Slow Food's argument is that there is no future for gastronomy without an awareness of the environmental context. The ecological focus is crucial in opening up gastronomy to the problems of globalisation and enables Slow Food to position its politics in ways that address the problems of environmental crisis, while shifting the focus away from the Western domination of traditional gastronomy. Vandana Shiva, Slow Food Vice-President, scientist and eco-feminist, has drawn on her involvement in the non-violent Chipko movement in the 1970s which opposed the destruction of forests, pointing out the contemporary links between environmental destruction and hunger.[15] Slow Food, like other environmental movements, is committed to *sustainability*, and has taken part in a range of initiatives on sustainable agriculture. Its biennial 'Slow Fish' event, a mixture of meetings and tastings, has warned of the crisis in the fishing industry and the real risk of fish species becoming extinct if we carry on consuming at the same rate. Slow Food has partly positioned its politics around the global contradictions between obesity and hunger, focusing on the excessive consumption and waste in the West and the need to develop local rural economies in the South. It shares this approach with other environmental movements. What makes Slow Food's philosophy unique is the amalgamation of the two concepts of gastronomy and ecology. It is partly summed up in their phrase 'mangiare meno e mangiare meglio' ('eat less and eat better'). Amalgamating the two concepts, according to Carlo Petrini, ends the 'fictitious separation' between 'subsistence' and 'pleasure', reconciles the pursuit of pleasure with the daily struggles of peasant farmers in the South, and reinforces the universal principle of the right to pleasure outlined in the Slow Food Manifesto.

Eco-gastronomy addresses the crisis of *biodiversity* that has seen certain animal breeds, plant varieties, types of cheese and cured meats all but disappear, together with the traditional peasant culture, heritage and knowledge that sustained them. The crisis, driven by industrial agriculture, including the use of chemicals, is now putting artisan food at risk. Multinational companies are compelling farmers to purchase their seeds on a regular basis, which, according to Slow Food, as well as increasing economic dependency and destroying local traditions, has a detrimental effect on the quality of food:

> In the demented drive towards a world of tomatoes that don't go bad and strawberries with salmon genes, indigenous species and varieties selected by tradition, their flavours and the opportunity (of which we have already availed ourselves in the past) of finding varieties resistant to the attack of certain parasites in the far corners of the earth are all being sacrificed.[16]

Maintaining biodiversity is essential for the future of the planet, which needs regional varieties and natural habitats, but it is also crucial for the preservation of pleasure. Eco-gastronomy therefore provides Slow Food with a politics embedded in local and global relations, and a deep critique of the current global system. As Parkins and Craig argue: 'The distinctive political identity of Slow Food stems from the "unusual" articulation of "gastronomy" and "ecology".'[17]

Unsurprisingly, as a distinctive political idea, eco-gastronomy has a new ideological appeal, with its emphasis on pleasure cutting across traditional distinctions of left and right. Petrini has argued that a 'gastronome who is not an ecologist is stupid, while an ecologist who is not a gastronome is sad'.[18] Slow Food's emphasis on pleasure distinguishes it from the puritanical nature of some environmental movements, while it also differs markedly from the frugality of other movements. Its preference for organic agriculture brings it closer to organisations like the Soil Association in the UK, though it does not accept the organic principle in all cases (for example in situations where excessive 'food miles' are involved). It also has reservations about the costs of organic accreditation schemes which often exclude small producers, notwithstanding the complexities and inconsistencies now associated with organic status, with no less than nine different certification agencies in the UK alone.[19]

Slow Food differs from the traditional movements of the left which have, in different ways, eschewed pleasure in the cause of struggle and commitment and perpetuated the mentality of the activist. It also departs from the top-down 'welfarism' of social democracy, which only forms an accommodation with capital within the constraints of a nation-state. Likewise, neo-liberalism is the focus of much of Slow Food's critique of the power of the global market and its effects on local cultures, working conditions and the environment. Forms of Christian Democracy do not sit easily with Slow Food's pleasure principle either.

Eco-gastronomy, then, presents a challenge to mainstream ideological traditions. This does not mean that Slow Food is an ideology-free movement. In fact, it is a very ideological movement, with clear principles, critiques, counter-arguments and holistic programmes. As we will see in the next chapter, it incorporates a systemic critique of the current world order ('fast life'), embodies alternative values, and envisages a different way of 'slow living'. Nor is it devoid of ideological influences from mainstream intellectual traditions. In fact it draws on aspects of traditional political thought in the hybrid, loose and fluid nature of political ideas in the late modern era. Indeed, while the food it favours is authentic, derived from long traditional knowledge and free of artificial chemicals and influences, Slow Food's ideological menu is distinctly nouvelle cuisine, a mix of previously incompatible ingredients. They have made digestible a set of ideas that previously had little appeal to the political palate, enabling the power of 'old ideas' to live in new settings. Some have argued that such a hybrid thought is a feature of the late modern age, but Slow Food's fusion is surely a unique combination, and made more complex by the ways in which its ideas have resonated with different national political traditions. Slow Food has also had particular points of arrival in different countries, where crises over food, health, or the environment have given added force to its appeal.

Thus the critical interpretation of capitalist development, according to the Marxist view – where the pursuit of greater wealth, profit and capital accumulation has exploited the natural resources of the world and the labour of workers and brought increasing inequality – is present and partly a legacy of the Italian Left. Slow Food's identification with the plight of small producers in the face of the global economy has some connection to this tradition, though its critique of 'standardisation', rooted in a distinctive politics of aesthetics, has more in common with the concern of John Stuart Mill, Alexis de Tocqueville and James Madison that individual choice and diversity would be suffocated under mass culture. However, whatever the inadequacies of his thought on an alternative society and the historic mission of the Western proletariat, Marx's thinking on the development of the global market remains pertinent in Slow Food's critique. Slow Food also had some close affinity with the critiques of the so-called 'anti-globalisation' activists, though it developed an increasingly different strategy.

The environmentalist strand became stronger as the movement developed a global political outlook from 1996 when the Ark of Taste was set up, and subsequently the Presidia (1999), the Foundation for Biodiversity (2003), and Terra Madre (2004). In Germany, according to Slow Food President Otto Geisel, the movement started in 1992 as a response to a greater awareness of the problems of industrialised food that had become dominant since the 1950s and a growing recognition that quality food need not be confined to the rich. The appeal, according to

Geisel – a gastronome who only uses food sourced within 50 kilometres of his Michelin Star restaurant – was partly influenced by a stronger awareness of environmental issues and the strength of the Green Party, and blended with some existing environmental initiatives. In Germany, for example, there is a strong school gardens movement involving 20,000 members and the attempt to reactivate school gardens has been an important element in Slow Food's educational activities having a strong appeal to prospective new members. This has also suggested a different weight in the balance of pleasure and environmental commitment than in the Italian case, though perhaps the distinction is also reflected in the different circumstances in which Slow Food grew in comparison to Italy. 'In Italy', Geisel told me, 'they had something to defend; their culture. We have to rediscover our food cultures.'

The green influence was particularly strong in the origins of Slow Food Germany but there were other influences, often shaped by regional as well as political factors. Lisa Engler, one of Germany's youngest convivium leaders, describes the politics of her convivium as 'a kind of melting pot, with every style of political background within the group'. If there was a slight left-green bias, this was compensated by some conservative influences. She does not see the combination of anti-globalisation activists and conservatives as contradictory. Different political backgrounds seemed less important than regional differences in some of the priorities of Slow Food in Germany. In the south of the country, the Italian influence in Munich and Stuttgart was important. In eastern Germany, the effects of communism still lingered and much emphasis was on rebuilding lost agricultural traditions, reviving areas polluted by heavy chemical factories and drawing on the knowledge of older people in Rostock and other areas. In the lake district of Mecklenburg, an isolated rural area with high unemployment, the high quality of natural resources surrounding the lakes and the national park were the basis for the redevelopment of local tourism.

Similar situations occurred in other parts of Eastern Europe, making it a growth area for Slow Food, under very different circumstances from those in the West. The development of Slow Food in places like Poland, Romania, Armenia and Belarus is rooted in the need to revive local economies by returning to traditional agriculture which had been ruined by communism, while resisting the challenge of the unrestrained global free markets from the West, represented by multi-nationals and fast food stores. In countries with few or no traditions of tourism and the availability of instant capital, the chances of developing a sustainable alternative were relatively low. The task was made more difficult by long-held suspicions of ideology and forms of association. Yet Slow Food, in alliance with other trusts and foundations, has been able to help revive local food in these places by a commitment to the producer.

Unsurprisingly, there is also a strong conservative element in Slow Food thinking, which laments the loss of traditional culture and is committed to the stewardship of the environment. 'Consolidated wisdom', based on learned experience, in Edmund Burke's view, and the importance of paying heed to tradition in making choices about food, are crucial to Slow Food's ideas and have a practical expression in the Ark of Taste and Presidia which aim to preserve lost tastes and rekindle traditional food cultures at risk of extinction. Slow Food's emphasis on tradition, however, is not, as is sometimes assumed, a nostalgic return to the past. Rather, Slow Food has drawn on traditions which provide knowledge of, and form identities around, food. These traditions are also indicative of specialised skills; indeed traditions start out as innovations. As the British food writer Matthew Fort puts it:

'It is a curious paradox, but every traditional dish, every time-honoured cooking technique, every artisan product, every Presidium and every Ark product, started off life as an innovation.'[20] Indeed, Petrini often quotes the food historian Massimo Montanari's belief that every tradition is 'a very successful innovation'.[21] When he repeated that view in a meeting with David Cameron, on the occasion of the launch of the UK Slow Food office in December 2006, the leader of the British Conservative Party wrote it down and promised to use it. This may be testament to the way the modern Conservative Party works, but the link with the conservative tradition is real.

In fact, one of the leading Slow Food advocates in the UK is 'Zac' Goldsmith, editor of the *Ecologist* magazine, who wrote the Conservative Party's key environmental policy document, 'Blueprint For a Green Economy' in 2007, and is the founder of FARM, an organisation which brings together farmers and environmentalists. However, Slow Food in Britain does not sit easily with the ideas of any of the political parties. It has little connection to New Labour's technocratic managerialism, while Slow Food's critique of global capitalism has yet to win friends amongst the more puritan and often anti-intellectual British Left, for whom the movement is still regarded as an elitist middle-class dinner club.

Despite the absence of the British Left from Slow Food, it is not difficult to find a radical edge to the movement in Britain. This radicalism, found in growing numbers of discerning consumers, can be understood to some degree as the critical voice of Middle England. This is not the Middle England immortalised by New Labour spin doctors, a rather static homogeneous entity, assumed to be *Daily Mail* reading, illiberal and intolerant. Rather it is a 'liberal' and enlightened Middle England, inhabited by people concerned about the environment and worried about education, who frequent farmers' markets and are convinced 'Italophiles'.[22] In his BBC Radio 4 series, 'Looking for Middle England', Ian Hislop visited Ludlow in Shropshire where he found the Ludlow Civic Society opposing housing development on green spaces and much evidence of a slower pace of life. Ludlow, the home of Slow Food UK, is a small town renowned for its restaurants, food festival and the quality of its local produce. At the annual food festival which attracts 50,000 people, Slow Food organises taste workshops in the Castle and the 'Magnalonga', a walk through the local countryside with local stops along the way for different courses of local food.

With a presence in the Scottish Highlands and mid Wales, perhaps 'Middle Britain' would be a more accurate term, but the heart of Slow Food in the UK is the rural shires. The Six British Presidia products, those deemed to be of exceptional quality and derived from artisan wisdom, knowledge and experience learned over generations, are located deep in the navel of middle England. They include 'Three Counties Perry', a drink made from fermented juice of bitter perry pears and produced in Herefordshire, Worcestershire and Gloucestershire; Old Gloucester beef, made from ancient and endangered traditional breeds; Artisan Somerset Cheddar, made from fresh local raw milk; Single and Double Gloucester cheese; Cornish pilchards and sardines produced since 1555 and mainly exported to Italy, but now down to its last single producer; and Fal River oysters from Truro.

With the exception of the cultural centres of London and Edinburgh where Slow Food has active memberships and close links with food writers and journalists (it has few members in the other main cities in Britain), many of its activists are dispersed in the shires of Somerset, Shropshire, Oxfordshire, Cornwall, Dorset, Cumbria, Norfolk, Bedfordshire and Gloucestershire. Started by Wendy Fogarty in London at the end of 1997, Slow Food increased its presence in Britain on the back of a response by growing numbers of critical consumers to a series of food crises and an increasing desire for improved quality of life. Along the way it has attracted some famous food writers and chefs, as well as self-taught gastronomes.

Slow Food in Britain has close links with the Soil Association and has a number of organic farmers amongst its members.

Prince Charles, who maintains an organic farm on his estate at Highgrove, Gloucestershire, has been a prominent supporter of Slow Food in the UK. His relationship with Carlo Petrini, the ex-communist seventies' radical, is one of the more interesting examples of Slow Food's ecumenical politics. Charles had been a keynote speaker at the first Terra Madre in 2004, and in 2007 sent a message of support to the Slow Food Mexico Congress (where he described Petrini as 'one of his heroes'). In recent years Charles has been an outspoken opponent of McDonald's and a frequent campaigner on numerous environmental issues, for instance calling on the UN to reduce greenhouse gases. In one of their meetings at Highgrove in 2007, Charles told Petrini of his dismay at the

> lack of connection with nature and the world around us – which has been causing such terrible damage, along with the loss of land ... Everything is wasteful – and ugly! What I cannot bear is the 'uglification' of the entire world and also the homogenization of the world. So, wherever you go, under the insane 'globalized' approach – because it doesn't have a human face, globalization – you might just as well be in the same country.

As Petrini departed, Charles shared his admiration for Italy's food traditions, notably for 'the way you treat food as an art form'.[23] In advance of the meeting he had asked Slow Food for advice on what to do with his pigs, possibly with the intention of producing salami.

Slow Food's diverse membership, drawn from a variety of like-minded people – gastronomes, producers, consumers, farmers, anti-global activists, environmentalists, chefs and fisherfolk from across the globe – is one of its unique features. As I will argue, some have become new political subjects. They have helped shape the ideas of the movement and in the process have challenged the authority of experts. This reflects the moment, which some have described as one of postmodern ambiguity, where traditional belief systems and experts have lost their authority in a period of uncertainty. It is not surprising that Slow Food grew in this era when the BSE crisis and the rise of GM crops forced many issues onto the agenda. Slow Food has put its faith in traditional knowledge, the artisan skills and wisdom of the producer, and the taste buds of the self-taught gastronome. In doing so it has had to challenge not only policy makers but the opinions of some food scientists and nutritionists. Michael Pollan, in his book *In Defence of Food*,[24] has argued that there is now an 'ideology of nutritionism', which has delineated 'good' and 'bad' ways of eating according to which chemicals are inscribed on the packaging, and where food has been reduced to 'medicine' or 'poison'. As such the pleasures and identities produced by food have been marginalised or forgotten.

Slow Food is an Italian movement which has attracted members from six continents in its attempts to reconnect people to the pleasures of food. Some have suggested Slow Food is not a political movement, perhaps mindful of the ecumenical nature of Slow Food's ideas and its difference from mainstream politics, or because of the difficulties in associating 'pleasure' with 'politics'. However, Slow Food proposes a challenging set of ideas which have put food at the centre of many contemporary concerns. During 2007, Carlo Petrini was courted by leaders of Italy's latest new political organisation, the Democratic Party, to be one of its figureheads; perhaps in itself a recognition of the impact of Slow Food. After allowing his name to go forward as one of the founding regional committee members (which led to claims that he had ambitions of being a future Minister of Agriculture), he subsequently withdrew his involvement, preferring to concentrate on his own movement.[25] His belief seems to be that politics itself, at a global level, now has need of the best values of the osteria: civilisation, conviviality and respect for local identity.

2

The Critique of 'Fast Life'

According to the Slow Food Manifesto:

> We are enslaved by speed and have all succumbed to the same insidious virus: Fast Life which disrupts our habits, pervades the privacy of our homes and forces us to eat fast food ... In the name of productivity Fast Life has changed our way of being and threatens our environment and landscapes. So Slow Food is now the only progressive answer.

THIS CRITIQUE OF FAST LIFE, written by the poet and writer Folco Portinari, was presented at the founding international Slow Food Congress in Paris in 1989 and has become the call to arms for Slow Food activists. It presents a bold interrogation of a way of living as well as a critical comment on the way in which our eating habits have been shaped by fast food. A longer original version was published in the left-wing *Il Manifesto* newspaper in November 1987, signed by a list of left-wing political and cultural writers and artists, including the playwright Dario Fo, and followed the demonstration against the new McDonald's sited near the Spanish Steps in Rome in 1986. Explaining the idea behind the Manifesto, Portinari told the journalist Gigi Padovani that he 'came up with the expression "fast life," which seemed to sum up all the daily rituals of which fast food was a part'.[1] The subtitle is also revealing: 'International Movement for the Defence of and the Right to Pleasure'.

The original version gives deeper insight into the critique of 'fast life' and includes the following:

> The culture of our times rests on a false interpretation of industrial civilisation; in the name of dynamism and acceleration, man invents machines to find relief from work but at the same time adopts the machine as a model of how to live his life. ... Against those, and they are in the majority, who can't see the difference between efficiency and frenzy, we propose a healthy dose of sensual pleasures to be followed up with prolonged enjoyment.[2]

The Manifesto puts forward a systematic critique of 'Fast Life', rooted in the contemporary world of globalisation and the information society, and denounces a *way of living* that has denied people the simple pleasures of life. It also suggests the need for a holistic alternative rooted in culture, which is not merely about food, and which will restore pleasure as a principle and a universal right. Ultimately it is a political statement, made more profound and digestible, perhaps, in the shortened version. The critique of 'Fast Life' resonates with other critiques of the pace of modern life, attributed to the development of globalisation and the information society. According to James Gleick in *Faster: The Acceleration of Just About Everything*:

> We are in a rush. We are making haste. A compression of time characterises life today. Airport gates are minor intensifiers of the lose-not-a-minute anguish of our age. There are other intensifiers – places and objects that signify impatience. Certain notorious intersections and toll-booths. Doctors' anterooms ('waiting' rooms). The 'door close' button in elevators, so often a placebo, with no function but to distract for a moment those riders to whom 10 seconds seems an eternity. Speed-dial buttons on telephones: do you invest minutes in programming them and reap your reward in tenths of a second? Remote controls: their very existence, in the hands of a quick-reflexed, multi-tasking, channel-flipping, fast-forwarding citizenry, has caused an acceleration in the pace of films and television commercials.[3]

Gleick's description of the pace of contemporary life and the increasing obsession with maximising the use of time addresses a whole range of social activities and circumstances. Carl Honoré, in *In Praise of Slow*, has also written about the 'cult of speed' and the multiple consequences this has brought for health, parenting, mind, work and social life. For him terms like 'fast' and 'slow'

> do more than just describe a rate of change. They are shorthand for ways of being, or philosophies of life. Fast is busy, controlling, aggressive, hurried, analytical, stressed, superficial, impatient, active, quantity-over-quality. Slow is the opposite: calm, careful, receptive, still, intuitive, unhurried, patient, reflective, quality-over quantity.[4]

Honoré quotes Klaus Schwab, the former president of the World Economic Forum, who argued that 'We are moving from a world in which the big eat the small to one in which the fast eat the slow.'[5]

The equation of 'fast' with economic efficiency is crucial to contemporary globalisation and Slow Food's critique of it and I will return to that shortly. There are, however, some fundamental transformations in the nature of time and space which are reshaping modern social structures. In his groundbreaking work *The Network Society*, Manuel Castells discusses the impact of time-space compression on global financial markets. It was now the 'speed of transactions' that allowed the 'circulation of capital': 'It is the speed of the transaction, sometimes automatically programmed in the computer to make quasi-instantaneous decisions, that generates the gain and the loss.'[6] We have to distinguish between 'timeless time', 'real time' and 'virtual time' according to Castells, who noted the huge effects this 'diversification of time' was having on work and on the economics of Western societies:

> What is at stake, and what appears to be the prevailing trend in most advanced sectors of most advanced societies, is the general diversification of working time, depending on firms, networks,

jobs, occupations and characteristics of the workers. Such diversity ends up, in fact, being measured in terms of each worker's and each job's differential capacity to manage time.[7]

What Castells calls 'timeless time' is shaped by the 'space of flows'. It is these 'flows' which 'induce timeless time'. Castells describes the 'relentness supercession of time as an ordered sequence of events ... Timelessness sails in an ocean surrounded by time-bound shores, from where still can be heard the laments of time-chained creatures.'[8] We are seeing nothing less than the 'annihilation of time', according to Castells. It is the network society, or what others call the information society, that has driven this new mode of economics, with real significance for contemporary lifestyles including work, communication, family life and identity. The information society represents a new epoch of the post-industrial age, as radical in its own way as the shift that occurred during the processes of industrialisation. Technology has changed the way people have access to knowledge. The phrase 'knowledge is power' has taken on a new and unsettling set of meanings in the information age, with the possibility of greater freedoms to travel, to accumulate wealth and to live more autonomous lifestyles. The information society is characterised by more flexible and unstable work patterns, by transformations in space and time and by an increasingly interconnected media. These transformations, in the words of Castells, have had profound consequences:

> shaking institutions, transforming cultures, creating wealth and inducing poverty, spurring greed, innovation, and hope, while simultaneously imposing hardship and despair. It is indeed, brave or not, a new world.[9]

One consequence of these changes was the focus on the knowledge economy by leading policy makers. For the optimists in Silicon Valley, say, or to the intellectuals and think-tanks close to New Labour, whose governments embraced the fast life and its modernising managerialist trajectories more than any other, the future offered seemingly unlimited opportunities for individuals and society to progress *if only* cultures and institutions could keep up. According to Charles Leadbeater, 'We are weighed down by institutions, laws and cultures largely inherited from the industrial nineteenth century; yet we confront a global economy driven by an accelerating flow of new ideas and technologies which are creating the industries and products of the twenty-first century.'[10] For Leadbeater, an associate of the think-tank DEMOS and sometime close confidant of ex-Prime Minister Tony Blair, 'knowledge capitalism is the most powerful creative force we have yet developed to make people better off'.[11] The 'heart of this knowledge economy', according to him, would be London and Los Angeles precisely because 'these are places where ideas and people [are] circulated at great velocity'.[12] It is the power of the global market, which, combined with policies of social inclusion in order to keep people 'up to speed' rather than being 'left behind', is to drive this new knowledge economy. But the knowledge economy, utilising technology and able to 'harness finance and social capital', also depends upon traditional knowledge, customs and habits being made redundant:

> Agrarian-based hierarchically governed and largely self-sufficient communities whose social structures have been legitimized by tradition and reinforced by religion are being transformed into mobile, globally interconnected, innovative, urbanized societies in which political activity rests on popular consent. ... New ideas and technologies drive out the old. But people's institutions and cultures change far more slowly than ideas, technologies and products. That is why we find it so difficult to cope.[13]

The main problem for Leadbeater and the other apostles of fast living is how to keep up.

This optimistic view of globalisation sees the 'fast lane' as the route to a more open, prosperous society and 'tradition' as merely a constraint on progress. 'Managing the risks' of the fast, global world is the main preoccupation, along with utilising technology to provide forms of inclusion and opportunity to greater numbers of people; an idea developed in the West would need to be extended to poorer countries for them to prosper. The knowledge economy itself would overcome the traditional distinction between mental and manual labour. This rosy picture of the fast life has many adherents in government and industry and has shaped the agendas of most Western countries.

If the world has got faster then, according to globalisation theorists, it has also got smaller. With power centred in large global corporations, and the workforce dispersed over different continents, globalisation is re-shaping the political world, with new global elites asserting power and influence and new global movements protesting against injustice. The world is getting smaller, with greater ease of travel, more homogeneity of lifestyles and consumption of the media. However globalisation is affecting the lives of people in different ways. The new global elites, based on spatial and global divisions, have been able to move around the world with ease, while capital knows no national boundaries. Others, by contrast, have been rooted more deeply into their own localities, trapped by the inequality of wealth and lack of resources. Globalisation may have brought new jobs but has also reinforced old divisions in new contexts. New informational hierarchies have created a gap between the 'information rich' and 'information poor'. While the jet-setting elites set the agenda, many communities in the world have never encountered a telephone.

This kind of optimism was at its height during the early 1990s, when liberal capitalism carried all before it, Francis Fukuyama proclaimed the end of history, and Eastern Europe was emerging from communism. In more recent times the costs of globalisation for the quality of life have been more apparent and the contradictions between economic growth and environmental catastrophe have threatened to become more intense. As we will see, the slow critique of the fast life focuses on these global inequalities and other costs of the fast information age. But it goes further than this. 'Fast Life' is synonymous with a particular view of globalisation, one which has imposed a *particular way of living*.

While globalisation may have brought evident technological benefits, increases in freedom and greater mobility for many, it has also meant privileging standardisation over diversity, and emphasised quantity over quality and the erosion of traditional knowledge in pursuit of the knowledge economy. Economic goals have come at cultural, environmental and architectural costs, as high streets, shopping malls and fast food outlets reflect increasingly homogeneous lives. Anglo-American cultural values have shaped the development of globalisation in particular directions.

According to Victoria de Grazia, globalisation should be understood as the 'triumph of American consumer society over Europe's bourgeois civilisation'. Her argument in *Irresistible Empire: America's Advance Through 20th Century Europe*[14] is that the American way of life, and its standard of living, achieved 'global cultural hegemony' during the last century as European lifestyles 'succumbed' to what she calls 'market driven imperialism'. It was the American ability to produce and market mass products, from the mindset of Woodrow Wilson in 1916 onwards, that drove this 'consumer revolution', according to de Grazia. It was a revolution which imposed new ways of living by removing barriers to elite tastes, allowing access to more and more goods and services and raising general standards of living. The consumer society broke down divisions of taste and distinction and was made possible by what de Grazia calls a 'new service ethic':

> How would consumer society as we know it exist without, say, the elaboration of a new ethic of service to make elites accept ... that barriers of taste had to be overcome, and that in principle the creature needs of those at the top of the social hierarchy were no different from those at the bottom?[15]

For de Grazia, by the end of the twentieth century this American vision had become a universal vision. Indeed the imposition of an 'American way of life' over European values suggests a way of living that penetrated all aspects of the society. One of the main features of globalisation in its contemporary and dominant forms, according to many, is the imposition of a standardised culture. The market provides access and opportunity but also excludes and imposes adherence to certain values. George Ritzer has described this process of standardisation as the 'globalisation of nothing', with particular significance for food:

> The nature of globalization, at least at its most expansive and intrusive, favors the worldwide distribution of 'nothing' in myriad ways, including and perhaps especially, food. The term nothing is used in this context in a very specific way to mean any social form ... that is centrally conceived, centrally controlled, and lacking in distinctive context.[16]

For the author of *The McDonaldization of Society*, the spreading of fast food outlets, Starbucks, Gap and other stores has led to a 'world of increasing homogeneity, a world in which virtually anywhere one turns one finds very familiar forms of nothing'. Ritzer contrasts this 'nothingness' with 'something', understood as that which is 'locally conceived and rich in distinctive context' and as a result 'far more difficult to distribute'. The implications for food are profound, according to Ritzer: 'It is not just that food is something that is unlikely to be much of a force globally, at least in comparison to nothing, but it is also the case that such food is threatened in its own local domain by the proliferation of nothing.'[17] This 'proliferation' has been made possible by the economic and cultural dominance of fast food chains and supermarkets, by major changes in the way food is produced and consumed, and by the way animals are raised and local traditions are eroded.

In the US, fast food became central in this way of life: it epitomised a way of living. Eric Schlosser, in *Fast Food Nation*, demonstrates evocatively the way fast food has become a dominant feature of contemporary American life.

> Fast food has infiltrated every nook and cranny of American society ... Fast food is now served at restaurants and drive-throughs; at stadiums, airports, zoos, high schools, elementary schools and universities, on cruise ships, trains and airplanes, at K-marts, wal-marts, gas stations and even at hospital cafeterias.

In 1970, Schlosser points out, Americans spent 6 million dollars on fast food; by 2001, this had grown to 110 billion dollars. This is more money than they spend on computers and new cars. 'More money is spent on fast food than movies, books, magazines, newspapers, videos and records combined.' The implications all this carries for health are now well known. More than half of all American adults and one quarter of American children are obese while about 30,000 Americans die each year because they are obese. In Schlosser's view, however, fast food has not only transformed the Nation's diet, 'but also our landscape, economy, workforce and popular culture. Fast Food and its consequences have become inescapable, regardless of whether you eat it twice a day, try to avoid it, or have never taken a single bite.'[18]

Supermarket chains are a further example of the way in which the production and consumption of food has become homogenised in the attempt to service the fast lives of consumers in the West. In her book *Shopped: The Shocking Power of British Supermarkets*, Joanna Blythman informs us that 80 per cent of food consumed in the UK is controlled by supermarkets, of which 70 per cent is in the hands of what she calls the 'supermarket superpowers' (Tesco, Asda and Sainsbury's). The effects of this concentration of power on the quality of life of British citizens has been far-reaching:

> The tentacles of this staggering concentration of power at the retail end of our food chain reach into all aspects of our lives. The look of our urban and rural landscape, the vitality of our high streets,

our reliance on the car, the nature and quality of the food we eat – all these have been profoundly influenced by supermarkets.[19]

Blythman describes the 'devastation' of this supermarket monopoly on Britain's independent traders, whom she calls the 'forgotten people' who have lost their businesses as a result of the expansion of supermarkets. Blythman reminds us of the scale of supermarket power since the 1950s when it had only 20 per cent of the market; now the situation has been reversed; the number of independent grocers slipped from 116,000 in 1961 to 20,900 in 1997, while the number of independent butchers has declined from 25,300 in 1977 to 8,344 in 2001.[20] 'The nation of shopkeepers', according to Blythman, 'has become a nation of supermarkets'. According to *The Grocer* magazine, 300 rural shops close down every year in Britain, while town centres, according to the New Economics Foundation, have been transformed into 'Ghost Towns', or what Blythman calls 'Trolley Towns', where the traditional 'sense of place' characterised by the distinctive architecture of local buildings has been replaced by a new corporate landscape. Blythman describes the gloomy picture encountered on entering one of these 'Trolley Towns':

> The first thing that greets you is not some distinctive civic monument or landmark but the now familiar supermarket sprawl, complete with its new roundabouts, altered road layout, traffic signals with changed priorities, petrol station and sea of parking. Welcome to Asdatown or Tescotown or Sainsburytown. Make it into the centre of one of these places and you're in Anytown, Anywhere.[21]

If we take the spread of fast food, the domination of supermarkets and the impositions of globalisation, then the 'Fast Life' that Slow Food opposes is a far-reaching and significant cultural phenomenon. It has not only speeded up economic transactions, forms of communication and modes of transport, it has also made the world smaller, more homogenised and standardised at one level, while sustaining global corporate elites at the other. Driven by a knowledge economy rather than relying on traditional forms of knowledge, it has increased the availability of goods and services, where the maximisation of quantity over quality has been justified by low-cost prices which work against the interests of local producers.

Slow Food's critique of fast food cannot therefore be separated from a broader critique of Fast Life, in which food becomes the key factor in a broader critique of fast living, with costs as diverse as poor safety and hygiene, obesity, poverty and famine, environmental degradation and global inequality. As Carlo Petrini and other Slow Food leaders have pointed out, Slow Food is not against *all* fast food. It is in favour of *fast slow food*, such as Roman street food, or the tortillas made by Mexican women from local ingredients and sold on the roadsides, or Kwei Tiew soup in Thailand, or Carangucijos crabs in Brazil or kefta in North Africa.[22] The difference lies in the culture which has shaped the preparation of this food. According to Portinari, there can be 'no slow food without slow life, meaning we cannot influence food culture without changing our culture as a whole'. Carlo Petrini also positions the politics of Slow Food within a wider cultural critique:

> Does the dogma of speed prevent us from pondering, tasting, comparing, and choosing? Better then to start with a slowing down, with a rhythm more suited to the training of the senses, to the calm perception of reality and tastes. Better to take more time to meet the producers, to do the shopping, to cook. Better also to 'waste' time – not in the sense of discarding it, like everything that is of no use to the disciples of speed – but by taking the time to think, to 'lose yourself' in thoughts that do not follow utilitarian lines: to cultivate the ecology of the mind, the regeneration of your existence. ...
>
> The quest for *slowness*, which begins as a simple rebellion against the impoverishment of taste in our lives, makes it possible to rediscover taste. By living slowly, you understand other things, too: by slowing down in comparison to the world, you soon come into contact with what the world regards as its 'dumps' of knowledge, which have been deemed slow and therefore marginalised. ... In coming into contact with this 'slow' world,

you feel a new (or renewed) relish for life, you sense the potential of different methods and forms of knowledge as counterweights to the direction currently being imparted in the tiller that steers our route toward the future.[23]

This perspective has become evident in the way local Slow Food groups present themselves to the public. In the USA, prospective members are asked to sign up to 'Slow Living': 'How to Live Slow' is the opening feature of the Slow Food USA website, which provides a list of ways in which people can change their lifestyles in order to enjoy food (from visiting farmers' markets, joining a community-supported agriculture scheme, taking time over lunch, shopping locally, starting a kitchen garden and paying fair prices). The feeling of meeting with like-minded people, as part of a movement, is evident.

The Fast Life has brought a particular mode of life under global capitalism; one which, according to Slow Food activists, has had a devastating effect not only on food, but also on landscape, community, biodiversity, local tradition and knowledge, the distinctiveness of taste, the environment and quality of life. The Slow Food critique of Fast Life can be described as holistic. While there is an overriding philosophical consensus that the simple pleasures of contemporary living are being eroded, its critique is more expansive and critically engages with the nature of globalisation. It cannot be reduced to a single-issue movement, a gourmet club, or an advice forum on how to eat healthily. Slow Food, in short, represents a critique of a *way of living*, which has brought it into many different political avenues and around which it has been able to build a significant movement on a global scale.

It differs from other movements by going beyond being merely oppositional and adopting instead a pre-figurative position, which attempts to articulate, in the conditions of the contemporary world, an alternative set of values that would facilitate the transformation of ways of living. The emphasis Slow Food puts on education, where members have the opportunity of sampling the good life and reviving the lost pleasures of eating in a convivial way, amounts to rethinking in fundamental ways the work–life balance. For its self-taught gastronomes, it offers, literally, the taste of a different kind of society. The idea of a local 'convivium', a Latin word used to denote a 'feast' or 'banquet', in place of the conventional party branch and defined by a commitment to pleasure as the organising principle of local activities, also challenges the practice of conventional political organisations. The *cittaslow* network, set up in Italy in 1999, was intended to create 'good living' in small cities (more familiar to Anglo-American readers as 'towns') of under 50,000 people. These towns promise 'good living' in which local communities are able to express their own local and regional identities through such things as the promotion of local hospitality, good eating and responsible tourism. In order to become a 'slow city', a strict set of commitments has to be met. These include an environmental policy which protects the local natural resources, encouraging the use of eco-friendly initiatives, preserving the typical produce of the locality, protecting local architecture and raising awareness amongst local citizens, through educational and public events, of what it means to live in a slow town.[24]

Wendy Parkins and Geoffrey Craig have defined the alternative way of living set out by Slow Food as 'Slow Living', one which has the capacity to challenge 'dominant narratives or values that characterise contemporary modernity':

> Slow living is not a counter-cultural retreat from everyday life. Slow living is not a return to the past, the good old days (pre McDonald's arcadia), neither is it a form of laziness, nor a slow-motion version of life, nor possible only in romantic locations like Tuscany. Rather ... slow living is a process whereby everyday life – in all its pace and complexity, frisson and routine – is approached with care and attention, as subjects attempt to negotiate the different temporalities that they daily experience; it is above all an attempt to live in the present in a meaningful, sustainable, thoughtful and pleasurable way.[25]

Slow living, according to Parkins and Craig, is about 'reclaiming time and pleasure' from 'hurry sickness', the centrality of work, and the erroneous equation of speed with efficiency. Slow living means a 're-evaluation' of the 'ethics of living'; slowness is 'a way of signalling an alternative set of values or a refusal to privilege the workplace over other domains of life. To declare the value of slowness in our work, in our personal life, in public life, is to promote a position counter to the dominant value-system of "the times".'[26]

'Slowness', in their view, is expressed in its most coherent form by the Slow Food movement, but is also, in some aspects, reflected by other organisations yearning for alternatives, ranging from the Voluntary Simplicity movement in the US to the 'wellness revolution', from the Society for the Deceleration of Time in Austria and the 'Take Back Your Time Day' in the US, to the growth of yoga and meditation classes. These initiatives have grown in response to the stress of work and 'time famine'.

A new 'ethics of time' is thus a distinctive feature of the idea of 'slowness'. Parkins and Craig see slowness as a response to the uncertainties and contradictions of living in what – from a cultural studies perspective – they call the 'global everyday' culture. They see slow living as an attempt to critically engage with contemporary life, a 'negotiation of the present', rather than a 'return to the past', one which addresses real processes of 'individualisation' in contemporary cultures. Parkins' and Craig's alternative 'ethics of time', based on redistributing and articulating different understandings of time, amounts to a way of living differently. The Fast Life's equation of speed with efficiency has meant less time for 'meaningful things' but now the possibility exists for the 'slow subject' to realise the 'ethical' potential of slow living.

To some degree a new ethics of time underpins Slow Food's particular form of alternative consumption. It shares with other movements, such as Friends of the Earth, Fair Trade and green consumer movements, a wider agenda of urging consumers to reflect on their own shopping habits. Whether through boycotting goods, consuming fair trade products or environmentally friendly goods, citizens have asserted themselves as critical consumers, influencing the marketplace in particular ways, by participating in politics and raising awareness of the origins or quality of food. This form of 'critical' or 'ethical' consumption has taken many forms, including boycotts, promoting fair trade, or advocating simpler lifestyles, 'symbolic campaigns' or 'discursive strategies'.[27] These have been categorised as 'negative' or 'positive' forms of consumption, depending on whether one is boycotting or buying, reflecting the traditional 'exit' and 'voice' distinction made by the economist Albert Hirschmann, between either rejecting the system (in this case the mass consumption movement) or seeking to participate in a different way, through 'alternative' consumption patterns.

The case of Slow Food reflects something of this shift while retaining a distinctive position. It partly reflects other forms of alternative consumption, whereby there is an attempt to influence ethical choices on which food to buy based on quality, the way it was produced, or because of the healthy ingredients. As with other types of alternative consumption, like fair trade or organic food, Slow Food consumers should be understood as concerned citizens sharing a broader set of values, such as commitments to justice, health and nature, which are often linked to particular lifestyles.

Yet Slow Food also differs from many other alternative consumption movements which, as Sassatelli argues, 'put prior emphasis on public values, such as the environment or human rights, safety and health ... [while] ... taste or refined aesthetic pleasure, do not appear to be primary concerns'.[28] For Slow Food, as we have seen, pleasure is a prior and essential element for the consumer. This distinction between Slow Food and other environmental and consumer campaigns implies a difference in strategy; it also reflects the distinctive cultural politics of Slow Food as it attempts to prefigure the possibilities of an alternative way of living.

Therefore while 'Fast Life', according to Slow Food, is synonymous with a particular type of globalisation, it is also indicative of a repressed idea of pleasure. Slow Food has emphasised the ways in which fast food has reduced eating to a functional activity, which shows little appreciation of different flavours and tastes, or spending time eating together, as part of a wider way of living which is uneasy with simple pleasures. This is particularly apparent in the US and the UK, the two countries most enamoured with fast food and which also have the highest rates of obesity, and the lowest annual holiday times, according to recent research.[29] In the US, fast food has also been shaped by the wider hegemony of the 'service ethic' (as de Grazia calls it), in which corporate and commodity values have become mainstream. This is reflected in attitudes to food where the check arrives before diners have ordered it, where waiters greet diners with a bland script of standardised phrases and little knowledge of the food they are presenting, and where the health warnings on wine bottles (for example to pregnant women) are more prominent than the details of the vintage. The service ethic was clearly a concern for the editors of the New York Slow Food restaurant guide, who felt it worth complimenting the waiters of Balthazar, a bustling Manhattan bistro, for their 'civil inattention'; one they define approvingly as 'a kind of laissez-faire attitude that allows your meal to be about you and not the quirks or games that people are often forced to play in the theater of fine dining'.[30]

In the UK, the phenomenon of 'binge drinking', where groups of men and women from all social classes drink quickly and act aggressively in towns and city centres, has grown to epic proportions according to recent research.[31] Equally noticeable has been the number of incidents resulting from British stag and hen parties held abroad, particularly in Eastern European countries that have been opened to Western tourists by low cost air travel.[32] At the beginning of January 2007 the British brewery chain Wetherspoon's introduced a rule forbidding adults with children from consuming more than two alcoholic drinks and requesting they leave the pub 30 minutes after finishing their meals, an outcome of particularly British attitudes towards pleasure. The idea that you can take pleasure drinking without getting drunk, a civilised value in the rest of Europe, remains anathema to mainstream British culture. According to the Slow Food critique, these are the results of a way of living in which instant pleasure is reduced to quantity rather than quality, uninformed by reflection or appreciation.

This argument has fuelled charges of elitism from critics of Slow Food. Part of this is due to the aesthetic emphasis on taste, where Slow Food, in emphasising quality of food is also, in effect, passing judgment on inferior tastes. The 'elitism' argument depicts Slow Food as an exclusive gourmet dining club, with a disdain for ordinary tastes (those of 'middle America' for example) and unrepentant about the fact that the costs of eating fresh organic produce are greater than the cost of shopping at supermarkets. Other critics accuse Slow Food of wanting to return to a nostalgic pre-modern era. Only the well-off have the economic means, time and flexibility of lifestyle to practice slow living:

> There is something rather sad about those people always banging on about the joys of Slow Shopping, and of its sister cousin Slow Food: it points to dull and dreary nostalgia-hounds with too much time on their hands and a morbid fear of modernity ... let them dawdle their day away over errands; but some of us love the buzz of getting things done quickly so we can move on and do something we love, be it sex or lazing away the day on the sofa or the beach with a good book.[33]

Slow Food's response has been that the cheap prices at Tesco's and other supermarkets (such as Carrefour or Wal-mart) are possible only because of the cheap labour they employ in the developing countries. In any case a lower percentage of

income is spent per household on food than in the past.[34] Nor is
spending time and money on food a rich person's hobby. Pierre
Bourdieu, in his study of taste amongst French social classes,
found that working-class families spent higher proportions of
their income on food (while the wealthier were more concerned
about health and figure) and enjoyed greater conviviality at the
table than the more sober, individualist middle classes.[35]

Accusations about lecturing the poor on their lifestyles have
been met with the Slow Food response that there are serious
health and environmental risks involved, and that changing
attitudes towards food and better lifestyles will only come
about through education. This is borne out partly by debates
over food and health in the US and UK particularly (though
the issue of obesity has been a problem facing all countries
in recent years, including Italy). After numerous schemes to
reduce obesity and change the eating habits of British school
children – including a well-publicised intervention by the chef
Jamie Oliver – had clearly failed, the Labour government took
the radical step in 2007 of instructing schools to warn parents
about their child's obesity. For Slow Food this confirmed the
view that the underlying problem was one of lifestyle, of a way
of living and of making the wrong cultural choices. John Dickie
in *Delizia*, his history of Italian food, argues that the underlying
principle of Slow Food is the Italian idea of 'civilisation of the
table', which is now gaining wider influence in the countries
where Slow Food has a presence.

> There is so much about the Slow Food movement that has its roots
> in Italy: its stress on what is simple and genuine; its pleasure in
> typical foods that express a sense of place and identity; its historical
> memory of plenty cruelly juxtaposed with hunger; its underlying
> belief in the sheer importance of eating.[36]

This 'civilisation of the table' Dickie sees as democratic and
egalitarian, in that a knowledge of food is held by Italians of
all social classes, in contrast to British or American teenagers
brought up on fast or packaged food. He records the series of

'horrors' that confront Italians when they come to Britain – fried breakfasts, eating on the move or on public transport, dishes that are defined by quantity even if it compromises flavour. The 'civilisation of the table', in Slow Food's discourse, has become a powerful message, one that reconciles politics with pleasure. Yet as Slow Food has grown into a global political movement, it has become apparent that this 'civilisation of the table' cannot be reduced to the dining styles of the affluent West, but must find a distinctive resonance with the economic predicaments of small producers in the South of the world, in their responses to the 'uncivilising' effects of the global economy.

3
Terra Madre

WE HAVE SEEN THAT Slow Food has a distinctive philosophy drawn from different intellectual traditions, organised around the idea of eco-gastronomy; that it has a critique of 'Fast Life' which embodies an alternative way of living; and that it holds a particular view of politics encapsulated by its pursuit of pleasure. This has given it an expanding profile as an association, but the major turning-point in Slow Food's development as a political movement came with the advent of Terra Madre, the 'World Meeting of Food Communities', first held in Turin in 2004. Terra Madre marked a significant watershed in Slow Food's approach as well as its public image and identity. Slow Food was now an aspiring global political movement which involved producers as well as consumers in its work, and was able to develop a distinctive position on globalisation. Its concepts – *Good*, *Clean* and *Fair* – became the organising principles for this new 'virtuous' globalisation.

The idea for Terra Madre was conceived by Petrini in discussion with his close associates following the first 'Slow Food Award for the Defence of Biodiversity' in 2000, in which farmers and small producers who had used traditional methods in defending a quality product had been recognised and rewarded. The awards ceremony brought together these ten or so producers, together with hundreds of journalists. With producers beginning to exchange experiences, Petrini had the idea of a much bigger project, an event which would bring together producers from across the world.[1] There was already an embryonic network of producers and food communities that had been put together over the previous two years following the formation of the Slow Food Foundation for Biodiversity in 2003, a project which required a lot of research, enormous work in building contacts, and a significant advance in the knowledge and expertise of Slow Food's international and scientific work.[2] The organisation for Terra Madre itself, headed by Paolo di Croce and Cinzia Scaffidi from the offices in Bra, entailed a large collaborative effort between the international office of Slow Food, local convivia, small producers, regional authorities in Italy and the local bed and breakfasts and farmhouses in Piedmont. With around 5,000 delegates from across continents, Terra Madre had a profound public impact not only within the Piedmont region, but also nationally in Italy, where it became a leading item on the news, while gaining wide coverage in the international press.

However, the main impact of Terra Madre was the transformation of Slow Food's politics. It brought together producers, farmers, consumers, intellectuals and activists from all corners of the world. The purpose was to 'meet, unite, exchange experiences and share their knowledge'.[3] The involvement of producers, notably those from developing countries, was crucial in shifting the attention of Slow Food from an association of gourmets to a political movement, with meetings on the future of food supplemented by calls for action on the environment, hunger and tourism.

Slow Food therefore had a new agenda and a new organising concept – the 'food community' – composed of producers and consumers brought together in a mutual dialogue. The producers were no longer peripheral to the sphere of Slow Food influence, but were regarded as increasingly important participants. As far as the developing countries were concerned, this was crucial; it was necessary to 'go beyond the celebration of poorer countries'. It was important that producers in the developing countries know 'that they are not alone'. The exchange between producers and consumers and others meant that the different elements of the food cycle were brought together. In the case of bread makers, for example, it would be farmers, those who bake bread and consumers.

Terra Madre provided a space for the movement to discuss and share views in a collaborative way. The significance of the issues discussed, such as the need for sustainable agriculture, the crisis in the fishing industry, and the plight of small farmers and producers, were questions of important public debate and as such attracted the attention of the press and involved politicians and government ministers, primarily in Italy but also beyond. Most of the speakers at Terra Madre 2004 and 2006 were on the left; yet the range of figures and personalities was broad enough to include both Prince Charles and Texan ranchers, while centre-right Italian administrations also supported the event.

Terra Madre was first held in October 2004 in Turin and brought together over 1,000 food communities on themes as diverse as biodiversity, hunger, poverty, sustainability, traditional food production, aquaculture, animal husbandry, the role of women in food production, and organic agriculture. There were workshops on 'Sustainable tourism', 'Defence and promotion of traditional beer styles', 'Non-timber resources of the Amazon forest' and 'Minor cereals: forgotten foods or foods of the future?' In attendance were 4,888 participants from over 130 countries, involving 1,200 different food communities. These included 257 food communities from Eastern Europe, 346 from Africa, 102 from North America, 273 from South America, and 224 from Asia and Oceana, in addition to those from Italy and Western Europe. The vast range of participants from different countries was seen as a major success for Slow Food, and Carlo Petrini, in his opening speech, could hardly contain his pride and emotion:

People are here from the Amazon jungle to the Chiapas mountains, from the Californian vineyards to First Nation reserves, from the shores of the Mediterranean, to the seas of Northern Europe, from the Balkans to Mongolia, from Africa to Australasia, all organised into what we have decided to call 'food communities'.[4]

Amongst the keynote speakers were Frei Betto, agriculture under-secretary to President Lula of Brazil. Betto took issue with Western approaches to aid, arguing that:

Famine cannot be fought with donations. There must be effective policies of structural change, including agricultural and fiscal reform, capable of demonstrating land rents and financial revenues. This must be supported by bold policies of investment and credit to families, who must also be assisted by an intense programme of education, according to the model of Paolo Freire, thus becoming socio-economic protagonists and political and historical actors.

Petrini had previously met with the Brazilian government, and contributed to President Lula's 'Zero Hunger' programme in discussions over sustainable agriculture. Another keynote speaker was Prince Charles, who had become interested in Slow Food through his involvement with the organic movement and his own experience on his organic estate at Highgrove, Gloucestershire. Charles, who has since kept up a regular rapport with Petrini (and praised in his speech the Slow Food president's 'unceasing energy'), had his own critique of the Fast Life, as driven by 'pure convenience' with damaging effects on community. His speech to Terra Madre in 2004 emphasised a specifically British emphasis on 'community' and 'rootedness', with perhaps an eye to Britain's long farming tradition. He shared the Slow Food commitment to biodiversity and sustainability. 'The Slow Food movement is about celebrating the culture of food and about sharing the extraordinary knowledge developed over millennia of the traditions involved with quality food production.'

The impact of Terra Madre on Slow Food's public profile and political identity was profound. It gained extensive media coverage and, in the opinion of the intellectuals associated with Slow Food, it was a unique occasion. Terra Madre was a

> living organism, created by men, women and communities whose livelihoods are threatened with extinction. Terra Madre brings together under one umbrella cultures that are far apart in type and distance, but suffer in common the impending menace of annihilation or extinction. For this reason it is neither a conference, nor a fair, nor a festival, but a coming to terms with and a binding of human efforts that express a daily need for contacts, complementary presences and exchanges of dialogue, products and foods.[5]

Terra Madre had a profound effect on the participants. Many of the small producers had never left their villages or regions before. Now they found themselves at the centre of attention in a new global movement. Slow Food and the Piedmont region had made a contribution to the transport and accommodation of the producers and provided hospitality and regional support. In general, the exchange between producers across different countries and continents was considered unique.

One of those inspired by Terra Madre was Maurice Small, a 40-something gardener and teacher from Cleveland, Ohio. Terra Madre, according to Small, was 'the fruit of the earth, where the people were the nutrients'. Speaking to me at his city farm in the centre of Cleveland, where he runs an educational programme for youngsters from deprived areas, Small said that he found Terra Madre 'a life-changing experience. When I got back, I spoke with the students and let them know that they were speaking with a new individual.' According to Samuel Muhunyu, leader of Slow Food Central Rift Convivium in Kenya, Terra Madre

> was a great inspiration for artisan food producers in Kenya. Through slavery, colonization and 'modernity' the African had come to accept and believe that their indigenous food culture was 'backward', 'primitive' and generally inferior. ... During Terra Madre and in subsequent Slow Food events, the Kenyan artisan food producers interacted with other food communities from all

over the world and realized how the others 'treasured' their food culture. This has greatly influenced positive thinking and they are becoming even more confident and proud about their own.⁶

In the view of the Slow Food leadership, Terra Madre was the beginning of the process of 'recognising' and 'acknowledging' the contribution of the producers.⁷ This was the new dimension in Slow Food's approach, which had shifted its emphasis from an association based in the Langhe part of Piedmont to an international movement. Terra Madre was also crucial in providing the catalyst for the development of new convivia, notably in the developing world. Some delegates returned to their own countries to set up Slow Food convivia. For the convivia leaders and delegates themselves Terra Madre opened up a whole new perspective for Slow Food. The emphasis shifted towards the global economy and the conditions of small farmers for whom they had developed a strong empathy.

In the run-up to the second Terra Madre in 2006, a more developed idea of the nature of the alliance between the different food communities and Slow Food was set out by the Slow Food leadership. While 2004 had given the limelight to the producers – the 'peasants, shepherds, breeders, gatherers, the guardians of ecosystems, large and small'⁸ – Terra Madre 2006 would give equal emphasis to cooks and academics. This would enable a new *network* to develop. Slow Food would now give political expression to this network by facilitating the dialogue.

According to Alberto Capatti, Dean of the University of Gastronomic Sciences, there were four fundamental 'forces' that would emerge at Terra Madre in 2006. First were the food communities who had come together from 'different areas of activity and social classes united by shared values and objectives', some of whom had remained in contact since 2004. Next were the chefs, the 'directors' of the kitchen, who nevertheless needed to learn the know-how of food production.

The Earth Workshops at Terra Madre would bring the chefs and producers together.

The third group were the university academics, whose role was to be the 'code-breakers, transmitters and reporters of the communities – the network through which, individual or sporadic connections apart, they could become interdependent'.[9] A new protocol between Slow Food and universities was agreed in October 2006, in which universities were able to state their allegiance by signing up to an agreement on support for sustainable agriculture and food.

The fourth dimension concerned the way in which the role of Slow Food was likely to change further by the impact of Terra Madre on its potential membership, one that would go 'beyond Western civilisation to embrace a varied culture formed of thousands of small individual communities'.[10]

The network envisaged by Slow Food distinguished it from other contemporary political movements. The alliance between producers, chefs and academics was more than a tactical alliance as found in other social movements, or a campaigning front, as with pressure groups. Nor, given the emphasis on promotion of local produce, was it a kind of fair trade or producers' association. The key to the network was the way in which the different kinds of knowledge and expertise of the three components complimented each other. According to Cinzia Scaffidi, head of the Slow Food Study Centre, there were three 'realms of knowledge': the traditional knowledge of the producer; the 'empirical knowledge of the cook'; and the 'scientific knowledge of the official researcher'. The key question, she argued, is 'how and to what extent could all these areas of knowledge interact in an egalitarian regime of sharing and interrelation?'[11]

This dialogue between realms was intended to transform the dynamics of the organisation of Slow Food, through equal respect afforded to the knowledge and expertise of the producers as much as to that of the academics. This effectively meant going beyond the divisions between mental and manual labour alluded to in different ways by Karl Marx, William Morris and Antonio Gramsci and the latter day theorists of the knowledge economy. The small producers, whom Slow Food has come to regard as the 'intellectuals of the earth', were the bearers of traditional knowledge, and their expertise and skills were fundamental to Slow Food's dialectic of change.

The network was also innovative in two other ways. First, the transformation in the relationship between the different realms would help project, in a holistic way, an alternative to the current food system, consistently represented as one in crisis. Second, the structure would need to be flexible enough to allow autonomy to the convivia and the food communities. According to Carlo Bogliotti, a close confidant of Petrini, the structure would allow the various convivia to relate to the food communities as 'nodes', by communicating important information sent from the centre to the local food communities. The Slow Food office would act as the 'engine and guarantor of the service', while key local roles would be carried out by mediators, normally convivium leaders, journalists, food community representatives or academics, whose central tasks would be to 'translate' messages from the centre 'into the language of their communities and convivia'. 'The mediator will act as a "postman" and use whatever means are available (fax, mail, hand delivery) to ensure every message reaches its destination.' These mediators, according to Bogliotti, would be the link between 'a number of network terminals', communicating amongst and within food communities (in 'mother tongue', to ensure 'cultural diversity') and 'documenting' the traditions and activities of the convivia. The mediators would have sufficient connection to the food community and culture to enable them to understand the local context and relate this back to Slow Food organisations.

This loose structure, Bogliotti argues, would enable Slow Food to respect the cultural diversity of its international membership and ensure that the relationship between the centre and the local organisation was dynamic and democratic: ' The network is shaped as a highly democratic tool and, as such, highly respectful of human diversity. And it is by believing in the power of diversity that we can obtain something creative and *good* [his emphasis] just as our philosophy demands'.[12]

The other central development to emerge from Terra Madre in addition to the network, was Slow Food's new principles of 'good, clean and fair' which had been set out in Petrini's book *Buono, pulito e giusto* in 2005,[13] and mooted by him in the documents which preceded Terra Madre. These were subsequently to become the organising principles of Slow Food's politics. These three principles gave a new clarity to Slow Food's objectives while connecting its philosophy to the wider movement.

By 'good', Petrini meant a commitment to quality, whereby food was assumed to be good based on the recognition of taste (including the level of sensory awareness, and allowing for cultural differences in taste), respect for nature, and the benefit to quality of life and a civilised society. 'Good' for Petrini meant 'good according to the palate and good according to the mind'.[14] It would be food that would enhance the 'reaffirmation of pleasure'. 'Good' also takes on a political meaning in the sense that it includes a respect for others and nature and will need to be defended if 'good, flavor, knowledge and pleasure are denied to us, withheld in the name of fear and offence or, more dangerously, in pursuit of profit'.[15]

The 'clean' principle was used to refer to the 'naturalness' in the way in which food was produced: 'A product is clean to the extent that its *production process* meets certain criteria of naturalness' (Petrini's emphasis). This raises the question of sustainability and knowledge of the way in which food has been produced: whether the soil has been polluted, what transportation is used, whether there are adverse affects on the environment through its consumption; in short the

'ecological consequences of the actions carried out during the
journey from the land to the table'. The industrialisation of
agriculture is for Petrini a key feature of the unsustainable
aspect of contemporary life. In order for a product to be 'clean',
therefore, the food must be 'sustainable' in its 'journey from
the field to the table'.[16] This is profoundly political, Petrini
argues, because of the need to reject the direction of the global
economy and the conflict between growth and sustainability. Petrini advocated the 'de-industrialisation' of agriculture,
which amounted to 'rejecting a system'.[17]

Finally, food that is 'fair' will have been produced in ways
that respect the work (both physical and knowledge-based
labour) through commensurate pay and conditions. It is a
commitment to social justice: 'It is not acceptable that those
who produce our food, those people (half of the total world
population) who work to grow crops, raise livestock and turn
nature into food, should be treated like social outcasts'.[18]
Fairness was thus linked by Petrini to 'social' and 'economic
sustainability', preserving the dignity of those who work the
land and a commitment to improving the social and economic
conditions of those in poorer countries. Indeed, the distinctiveness of Slow Food's new 'good, clean and fair' philosophy
seems to lie in the combination of its application to a range of
contemporary concerns, including the environment, fair trade
and quality of life, while remaining grounded in a systemic
critique of the global economic system. It is an idea of political
transformation with a series of practical and local initiatives.
'We can't change the world ourselves but we can contribute
to changing the world', Carlo Petrini has stated, and Terra
Madre, as Slow Food's biggest political gathering, reflected
the extent of its ambition.

The organisation for the second Terra Madre of 2006 was
more ambitious in scope. Not only was there a more clearly
defined idea of the purpose of Terra Madre but a significant
increase in participants with the higher attendance reflected

in more academics and cooks. In all there were 1,583 food communities, 4,803 producers, 953 cooks and 411 academics, plus 2,320 observers from 148 different countries. The event was organised with the help of 776 volunteers, while more than 1,000 locations throughout the Langhe region supplied hospitality for the participants. The event was opened by a choir of former peasant women from Emilia Romagna, dressed in traditional clothing. Their songs both evoked the memories of their struggles as rice growers, as well as empathising with current struggles against global capitalism.

The opening procession which followed gave the impression of a mini Olympics, as selected representatives of the different nations carried their national flag to the sound of Edward Elgar. Following the choir, the varied choice of music seemed to embody the very different cultural and political composition of those attending. Led off by Afghanistan and Albania, the biggest cheers were for Cuba, Lebanon, Palestine and the Native Americans. Indeed Sergio Champarino, Mayor of Turin, praised the 'Olympic spirit' of the occasion in his welcoming comments. The election of a centre-left government in Italy six months previously had some implications for the keynote speakers, who were all keen to link their policy agendas with the cause of Slow Food. The event was officially opened by Giorgio Napolitano, the President of the Italian Republic, while Massimo D'Alema, Deputy Prime Minister and Foreign Secretary, and Fausto Bertinotti, Speaker of the Chamber of Deputies, and Italy's leading communist, also made contributions.

In his opening speech, Carlo Petrini used the metaphor of 'Mother Earth' to set out the context of Terra Madre and the priorities of 'harmonising' the local economy with nature. 'We have prepared and fertilised the land. Honest land is ready to receive the seeds ready for Terra Madre. What is the distinctive seed of this meeting? The nomads, fishermen and farmers. The strong seeds of Terra Madre are the local economies.'

His speech outlined what he saw as the 'dramatic' failures of global capitalism to solve the pressing problems of the planet. Instead, it had brought loss of biodiversity, the destruction of ecosystems and the imposition of industrial agriculture over local traditions. He called for a new dialogue, a 'dialogue between realms', between science and traditional knowledge, a relationship that had broken down in recent years. The market economies of the North had wrought havoc on the local economies of the developing countries of the South. Indeed, those of us in the North, he argued, are 'accomplices' of the situation in the developing world, where there seemed to be no limits to consumption. 'How can we be the protectors; we are accomplices.' Indeed, since the North had created the problem, it was to the food communities of the South that we now had to turn. Petrini cited the different examples of farmers from green California and India, arguing that we must 'give back' the economy to farmers. This would be the focus of Terra Madre; it would provide the seed of 'virtuous globalisation'.

Aminata Traore, president of the African Social Forum, talked of the impact of war and hunger on her continent. She spoke of the destruction of the food and farming communities in her own country (Mali) and argued that food should be seen as 'welcoming' rather than as a weapon with which to bargain away people's future. 'Mother Earth is still rich enough for all of us', she declared. In the course of her speech she alluded to the plight of poor cotton farmers who had emigrated from Mali, only to die at Lampedusa, the small island off Sicily, attempting to embark in Italy. This was one of the pernicious effects of globalisation, which forced farmers and producers to move because their product was not paying enough for them to live on.

Kamal Mouzawak, who had set up the first Slow Food convivium in Lebanon, spoke of the realities of organising a farmers' market in Beirut, in an area affected by landmines. He saw the market as a meeting point for citizens and farmers.

During the Terra Madre sessions there were dinners and events which brought together both sides of the Palestinian divide. From Belarus, one of the Eastern European countries where Slow Food has a growing presence, Igor Danilov told delegates of the way in which Slow Food had helped revive 'forgotten crops' and restore traditions in opposition to the 'counterfeit' market which threatens to take people away from the land. He ended with a call: 'food producers of the world unite'.

There was one underlying argument in all these speeches: the global economic system is failing the peoples of the South, the environment and the local economy. Hope lies with investing resources and empowering the small producers of the South. The sheer breadth of producers, many dressed in traditional costume and leaving their localities for the first time, was apparent in the informal meetings and discussions. The more formal meetings involved local food communities and brought them into contact with other producers, cooks, chefs and consumers.

This went some way towards Slow Food's main objective of creating a global network between academics, chefs and small producers. This was evident in the packed US 'regional meeting' of Slow Food activists. This was the first time that different convivia, small producers from across the US, journalists, academics and chefs, had got together in one room. In all there were around 100 US cooks, 500 small producers and 100 convivia leaders from the US at Terra Madre. The sessions included films, personal reminiscences of Slow Food stories and very political speeches, from convivium leaders, producers, journalists and academics.

Alice Waters, after being introduced by Erika Lesser as a 'visionary leader', revealed during her speech Slow Food USA's intention to organise a major event for 2008. This was to be called Slow Food Nation and it would place SFUSA 'at the heart of the counter-culture of America'. It would be held in San Francisco, Waters' base, and would have a $2.5–3 million budget. According to Waters, it would be 'the coming of age for SFUSA'. A recurrent theme of the speeches was how to turn SFUSA into a political movement. According to the food writer Michael Pollan, the media still perceives Slow Food as a 'dining club', partly because pleasure and politics are viewed as 'diametrically opposed'. On the contrary, Pollan argued, Slow Food's potential as a 'political movement' is clear from its commitment to 'virtuous globalisation' and 'eco-gastronomy'. The task of Slow Food USA was to put itself at the centre of debates about food, including the disparity between obesity and scarcity.

This was a theme taken up by David Masimoto, a farmer who asked: 'is there a collective story for action and political change?' 'While we have memories of food, do we also have memories of food as a political force?' In fact delegates heard recounted stories of practical examples where Slow Food USA had intervened politically on major issues of food politics. One such example followed the aftermath of Hurricane Katrina when many businesses in New Orleans had been left ruined. Poppy Tooker from New Orleans discussed the way her 'food culture was threatened' and how 'the Slow Food nation' helped her to recover. Kay and Ray Broadhurst, shrimp farmers from the city, had lost their boat in the storms and their business was wrecked. With the help of Slow Food, and the efforts of the convivium leaders to raise money, the boat was rebuilt and six weeks later they were able to re-start their business.

Speakers urged their comrades to get organised ('Why aren't we doing this at home?' asked Deborah Madison), and go to San Francisco for Slow Food Nation, planned as a 'landmark' and 'watershed' moment on 'home territory'.

Terra Madre transformed Slow Food's politics and has shaped its development as an emerging global movement. Fausto Bertinotti, then speaker of Italy's lower Chamber of Deputies, said it reminded him of the World Social Forum assembly in Brazil. He predicted a 'new era' and 'new hope', one characterised by the 'rebirth of lost populations and lands'. Farmers, according to Bertinotti, 'speak a universal language which all of us can learn from'. Vandana Shiva contrasted the world of 'Washington fiction' and 'the values of Monsanto' with the unique alliance that Terra Madre had initiated based on a defence of the local through global alliances.

Terra Madre had established a network which not only created more exchanges between producers but also organised smaller events along similar lines. In 2007, Brazil Terra Madre brought 250 delegates, 77 producers, 26 cooks and the involvement of academics from 9 universities. Two hundred journalists and observers were present and in addition to meetings and exchanges, fund-raising dinners and taste workshops, there was also a meeting between the Brazilian Ministry of Agriculture and Slow Food, the two organisers of the event, which also had the support of the Ferra nacional de Agricultura Familiar and Reforma Agraria. The 'gastronomic space' introduced the public to the Presidia products, and other Brazilian foods.[19]

Smaller Terra Madre events during 2007–8 were held in Belarus, Sweden, France and Ireland. Towards the end of 2007, convivia in the UK organised a series of Terra Madre dinners in support of small producers in Gabon, the UK Terra Madre delegates having been twinned with that country. The dinners were the first step towards 'creating a partnership with Gabon to support their projects'. 'Diners across the UK', the UK Slow Food office announced, 'will have the pleasure of discovering new flavours, tastes and traditions and, at the same time, give invaluable support to SFUK and Terra Madre'.

This combination of the traditional Salone del Gusto (Halls of Taste), which had been a feature of Slow Food's events every two years since 1996 (though only open to the public since 1998), with the Terra Madre gathering of producers maintained the crucial link between pleasure and responsibility. In 2006

150,000 people went through the gates in Turin and sampled a range of products, including the many Presidia products which had been designated high quality, and in need of protection and investment. The conviviality of this event was such that tastings and dinners further enhanced the network by introducing new flavours, ideas and experiences, while reinforcing the public face of Slow Food as a site of enjoyment and pleasure to a large number of people. Many smaller versions of the Salone have taken off in different countries, including Fertile Ground and Urban Harvest in the US, the Aux Origines du Goût in France, the Deutscher Kasemarkt in Germany and the Barossa Slow event in Australia. The rows of food and drink on display at all these events suggest an alternative to the mass columns of supermarket shelves. It was as a result of the success of the Salone in Turin that *Eataly* was first established in the city, effectively as an alternative supermarket of local home-grown produce. A second store was due to open in Manhattan shortly after.

Since the first Terra Madre, Slow Food has attempted to ground itself in the experiences, culture and traditions of the producers. This gives it a different dimension from many other consumer associations and movements, while also distinguishing it from other anti-global political movements by virtue not only of appealing to and acting in solidarity with producers, but by positioning their work and livelihoods as central to the dynamic of change. This emphasis on the producing class may have some similarity with the left parties and movements of the past. Slow Food identifies, however, primarily with agricultural workers, and sees a new 'rurality' rather than the proletarianisation of the industrial workers as the basis for social change. In doing so, Slow Food can claim to be a uniquely global movement which, through the network which first came together at Terra Madre, has attempted to move beyond the standpoint of opposition in attempting to articulate an alternative idea of globalisation. Terra Madre provided the impetus for exchanges and projects as well as distinctive new voices. Indeed, amongst critical-ethical consumers, and, increasingly, amongst producers themselves, the 'intellectuals of the earth', as well as cooks and chefs, it heralded the arrival of new political subjects.

Part Two
People

4

Gastronome! The Arrival of a New Political Subject

H E MAKES FOR AN unlikely political actor. Approaching 60, bearded, tie-less and free of the usual politician's language of restraint, compromise, and 'the national interest', he talks, without notes, of the 'universal right to pleasure', the 'law of the stomach', 'virtuous globalisation' and the 'dialogue of realms'. However, be in no doubt: the message is serious, the cause is global, and the movement he represents is profoundly political. We are witnessing the arrival of a new political subject. The time of the gastronome is now upon us.

As the founder and international president of Slow Food, Carlo Petrini has become the most celebrated gastronome of his era. Only in more recent times has he been seen in any way as a major political figure. Yet his public recognition as a gastronome is a consequence of his own distinctive style of politics. His earlier experiences in Bra, as a local councillor, as the organiser of the *Cantè i'euv* festivals, the 'Free and Meritorious Association of the Friends of Barolo' and Arcigola, gave him a deep political and cultural insight – an apprenticeship in the 'politics of pleasure' – that has, together with more recent interest in ecology, helped shape his identity as a gastronome.

Like Slow Food's other leading gastronomes, Alice Waters and Vandana Shiva, Petrini has not compromised on the key principles. Alice Waters, the former sixties' Berkeley student, who carried her idealism into the principles which have sustained her restaurant, Chez Panisse, sees food as the key to changing culture. Food is about 'opening up the senses, seeing the world around you. It can be a strong moral and political force for change.' Vandana Shiva, the eco-feminist of the 1970s, sees a continuing contradiction between economic globalisation and the ability to provide enough quality food on the planet. The global economic system, she writes, 'is incapable of producing safe, culturally appropriate, tasty, quality food. And it is incapable of producing enough food for all because it is wasteful of land, water and energy.'[1]

Petrini himself is clear about his identity:

> I am a gastronome. No, not the glutton with no sense of restraint whose enjoyment of food is greater the more plentiful and forbidden it is. No, not a fool who is given to the pleasures of the table and indifferent to how the food got there. I like to imagine the hands of the people who grew it, transported it, processed it, and cooked it before it was served to me.[2]

The modern gastronome is, then, someone who will have a cultural awareness, and a global perspective, as well as be capable of a fine sensory analysis. As Petrini points out in his book, *Good, Clean and Fair*, today's gastronome is a figure who can move seamlessly across the different spheres of the world of food. The new gastronome is the pivotal figure in helping us understand critical discussions about the ecological and global economic context of food. The gastronome is someone who has 'a finely tuned sense of taste', but also a 'knowledge of food production that makes him care very much about the world around him'. Drawing on his own experience as a gastronome, Petrini perceives his role and that of others as a 'quest for culinary pleasure', with the knowledge 'that there is also a different world of production and consumption, parallel to the dominant one, which contains the seeds of a better global system'.

The modern gastronome is not simply a food expert, someone who reads books about food or eats in fine restaurants, but someone with an empathy for those who work on the land and who will increasingly need to engage with urgent environmental and economic questions. This is significantly different from the original meaning of 'gastronomy' when the term was first used in French in a poem by Joseph de Berchoux in 1800.[3] In post-revolutionary France gastronomy was part of the coming of age of the French bourgeoisie, giving birth to a new gastronomic literature and helping good food and restaurants gain cultural prominence for the emerging elite. There are still remnants of its original meaning that apply today. Jean Anthelme Brillat-Savarin, in The Physiology of Taste, written in 1825, defined gastronomy as 'the intelligent knowledge of whatever concerns man's nourishment'. He also perceived its 'interdisciplinary' nature, arguing that gastronomy incorporated natural history, physics, chemistry, cookery and business. Crucially, it also included political economy, because of the exchange and revenue created. Indeed, Petrini, in Good, Clean and Fair, sets about updating Brillat-Savarin's definition, in order to include sustainability, pleasure and fairness. He writes:

> Gastronomy is the intelligent knowledge of whatever concerns man's nourishment: it facilitates choice because it helps us to understand what quality is. It enables us to experience educated pleasure and to learn pleasure-loving knowledge. Man as he eats is culture: gastronomy is culture, both material and immaterial. Choice is a human right: gastronomy is freedom of choice. Pleasure is everybody's right and as such must be as responsible as possible: gastronomy is a creative matter, not a destructive one. Knowledge is everybody's right, but also a duty; gastronomy is education.[4]

Petrini argues that the interdisciplinary dimension identified by Brillat-Savarin has been maintained in modern gastronomy, now covering botany, physics, ecology, anthropology, geopolitics, cooking, political economy and technology. This interdisciplinarity was a distinctive feature of the new gastronomy and is reflected in the curriculum of the University of Gastronomic Sciences, set up by Slow Food in 2004. The university was formed to recognise gastronomy as a distinctive discipline in its own right, indeed as a 'science'. A student at the University of Gastronomic Sciences can expect to study courses on food history, gastronomic tourism, sensory evaluation, the sociology of consumption and the geography of wine, amongst others. The idea in providing students with a 'gastronomic education' was to

> help create a new type of professional; an expert who is able to lead and elevate the quality of production, to teach others how to taste, to guide the market and to communicate about and promote foods and beverages. In a world where 'specialities' and 'typical local products' are increasingly important and are raising the standards of the market, gastronomes will be able to communicate a wealth of knowledge, in advising new businesses, designing distribution outlets and advising the restaurant trade.[5]

The gastronome, according to Petrini, has now come of age, and today's gastronomes are not only graduate professionals of the university, but those deeply involved in different aspects of the world of food. Since the 1950s the issue of diet and quality of food has been a much broader concern which has attracted a new cohort of 'unconscious' and 'involuntary' gastronomes, according to Petrini, who have sought access to natural products in a world dominated by fast food and 'soul-destroying' supermarkets. According to Petrini there is a sharp contrast between the gastronome and the gourmet. The increase in food programmes on TV has brought more attention to food, but the obsession with recipes, media celebrity and reality TV has trivialised the more important questions and has not contributed significantly to counter the proliferation of 'bad food'. The difference between a gourmet and a gastronome, according to Petrini, is that the latter has a more profound and holistic understanding of food in a global context, while the former's commitment to taste is not matched by global or environmental awareness. The new gastronome unites the two principles of pleasure and ecological conscience.

This is why the intervention by British TV chef, Jamie Oliver, was warmly welcomed by Slow Food. From his first intervention on the mediocre quality of British school dinners, where he exposed the poor diet of Britain's children, to his later series on the conditions of battery hens in 'Jamie's Fowl Dinners' (2008), Oliver's distinctive contribution was to bring the attention of the British public to the whole process of food cultivation, transport and consumption, and, finally, taste. His programmes involved interviews with parents, producers and a variety of consumers. His first series led to a major public debate on school dinners which led to change in government policy, though to date it has not achieved a major success in changing the habits of British school children. His second series got him into hot water with Sainsbury's (one of his employers) after their own standards came under scrutiny, and suggested some contradictions in his role. The educative role of the programmes, however, influenced public debate about food in Britain and, in the case of the second series in particular, re-focused attention on the processes of production. While Oliver came in for some criticism from those who interpreted his programmes as indicative of a rich elite lecturing the poor about their eating habits, and others reducing his intervention to that of a new breed of moral food guardians, he seemed to touch the conscience and taste buds of a significant part of the nation, if the resulting dip in sales of factory farm chickens is anything to go by. At the same time, in confronting politicians, experts and farmers, he brought another dimension to the new role of the gastronome as a political subject.

Obviously Jamie Oliver has the benefit of regular access to the mainstream media well beyond the reach of the growing number of self-taught gastronomes, but his philosophy is in harmony with Slow Food's commitment to the producer. Indeed Petrini sees gastronomes as 'co-producers', such is their

knowledge and awareness of the whole process of cultivating
and producing food. The gastronomes who lead Slow Food
will be able to articulate their understanding of what is meant
by 'good, clean and fair'; they will be aware of the ecological
and economic context in which food is produced, and will
empathise with the plight of the small producer and support
their livelihoods and to intervene where issues of social justice
and environmental sustainability are under threat.

According to Petrini's criterion, then, a gastronome is
someone who combines environmental concern with the pursuit
of pleasure; an enlightened citizen who will have an expanding
knowledge of food in its social and environmental context and
an understanding and empathy for the predicaments of the
small producer in the era of globalisation. The gastronome
seeks an 'educated pleasure', one which carries a responsibility
to intervene on food issues and facilitate an understanding of
the processes of discovering, producing and enjoying food.

It is these values that have begun to unite gastronomes across
continents in the local convivia which serve as Slow Food's
equivalent of the party branch. There are currently 1,003
convivia worldwide, with over 400 in Italy, 170 in the US,
68 in Germany and 48 in the UK. In Italy, the 'condotte', as
convivia are known, have a presence similar in density to the
old party sezione or branches, with 39 in Tuscany and 38 in
Lombardy alone; a greater spread than the local organisation
of the new Democratic Party.

These convivia organise a range of educational and other
cultural events in order to promote local produce and the
'gastronomic dignity' of the producers. Some convivia,
particularly in Western Europe, are composed mainly of 'critical
consumers' in support of producers; others, including those in
Eastern Europe, where attempts have been made to rebuild food
cultures as an urgent economic priority, were founded through
work with producers. Some convivia in Africa, central America
and India were founded following Terra Madre. Therefore some

convivia have closer links to local producers (in a minority of cases the producers are convivium leaders), and base their events around their produce and circumstances; others are more detached and focus on tasting and education. There are also significant differences in priorities in rural and urban areas as well as significant national and cultural differences between convivia, which may have specific political and historical contexts shaping their activities. Unsurprisingly perhaps, where there is greater geographical distance between one convivium and the next, there is more reliance on Internet communication. In the US in 2008 around 90 per cent of convivia have their own websites, whereas in Italy, where there is a higher density of convivia, 90 per cent (in the two biggest regions Tuscany and Lombardy) are without their own website.

There are also significant differences in the ways in which convivia appeal to their members or prospective members. Slow Food San Diego's website, for example, is very up front about reasons why people should join Slow Food:

'Why You Should Join Slow Food San Diego'.
1. Slow Down. Enjoy family, friends, meet new like-minded people.
2. Social Action. Once you've gotten together ideas will flow about how to help the community ... Slow Food San Diego is committed to awakening young people to the enjoyment and health benefits of wholesome food. The sustainable farm is successfully reaching teens about ecologically sound food production while giving them a sense of positive accomplishment through land stewardship.
3. Local Food Network. There are Slow Food conviviums around the world. When you travel, you're part of the international slow food movement, so you're never alone if there are 'slow foodies' at your destination.[6]

Convivium leaders also come from a range of different occupational backgrounds. Amongst those I interviewed, leaders included an occupational psychologist, a pharmaceutical employee, hoteliers, food writers, journalists, public sector employees, wine distributors, a stockbroker, chefs, farmers and a delicatessen owner. Most were in professional jobs which might explain the flexibility they had in putting in very long hours for their Slow Food work, as well as the good access to the media many enjoyed, while the involvement of restaurants and local shops in Slow Food events was often based on their local knowledge and contacts. Their political backgrounds varied and included most shades of political sympathy with a small bias towards the green/left positions. All have problems attracting younger members while there are some significant differences in the distribution of men and women amongst convivia leadership, with the US and the UK having significantly more women convivium leaders than Italy for example.

Few of those I have spoken to, however, had been involved in formal politics or campaigns of any kind before joining Slow Food, though in Italy more had some connections with movements or parties and a good knowledge of Italian politics. Ulrich Rosenbaum, the Berlin convivium leader and editor of the German Slow Food magazine, listed a range of political affiliations among his membership (including some senior Christian Democrat, Green Party, and ex-communist members), while his work as a journalist gave him good access to politicians. But even in this case, most Berlin members were relatively new to any form of political involvement and attracted to Slow Food by the chance of enjoying a good meal. In general the convivium leaders were the ones who were more likely to have read Carlo Petrini's latest book or article, heard him speak, and be more aware of the international nature of Slow Food than the ordinary member. This is similar to other movements, though unlike many movements where grassroots members put pressure on their leaders, Slow Food leaders often seemed to be politically more radical than the ordinary member, urging more activity and change in approach, particularly as the movement continued its shift from classical gastronomy to a more political position.

The type of events convivium leaders organise varied according to local culture, the strength of the relationship to producers, whether the balance was tipped towards 'classic gastronomy' or environmental politics, and whether they were located in urban or rural places. Events included wine tasting, 'meet the producers', visits to farmers' markets, food walks, fund-raising dinners, celebration of Ark or Presidium products, visits to school gardens, a book club and campaign meetings.

The leader's role is similar in some ways to that of a party branch secretary, who maintains the minutes, reports on meetings, supervises the membership and work of the party or movement, and takes initiatives on campaigns. Convivium leaders do much of this, aided by a convivium committee, which will include a treasurer, secretary, and possibly a webmaster and events organiser, but they are often also 'mediators' between the national and international movement and the locality, liaising with small producers and restaurants. Perhaps the biggest difference between them and other local political organisers is that they also have a responsibility to promote conviviality and pleasure, with all the costs and complexities of negotiating with producers that involves. Some convivium leaders told me that for some members, who joined primarily for the opportunity to eat good food and enjoy fine wine, the more political shift has been too much. Some have resisted the shift, while others have become 'politicised' by the more global expansion of Slow Food's outlook in recent times. Those who attended Terra Madre have found the evolution of Slow Food's politics easier to accommodate.

Few of the convivium leaders I spoke to openly identified themselves as gastronomes – hardly surprising, perhaps, given the cultural assumptions of elitism that pervade many attitudes towards food. However, given Petrini's characterisation, the roles they have taken on, their critical engagement with the state of food cultures, and their empathy with producers and more global outlooks, all suggest that we need to recognise the arrival of the gastronome as a political actor in the 'unconscious' or 'involuntary' way he suggested.

In the Swiss Alps, 1800 metres above sea-level, Marc Aerni, leader of the Engadine Valley convivium, and a hotelier in Zuoz, a village of less than 1,000 people, told me why he became involved in Slow Food. He was originally attracted to the idea of helping third world farmers protect their products. For him this idea was strengthened by the experience of going to Terra Madre in 2004, after which it 'had become a much deeper conviction than before'. Now his convivium organises visits to local farmers to get to know the problems they face, particularly in remote areas.

Aerni's role as convivium leader comes close to Petrini's idea of a gastronome by his concern for an educated pleasure. Through 'what I produce and through what I give to my guests, I try and live this slow food idea, using local products from the area.' He places Slow Food literature amongst the other tourist brochures in the hotel. For Aerni, a Slow Food presence in schools is vital. Two of his members are teachers and he sees educational projects as crucial in warning future generations of the consequences of the standardisation of food which he regards as a major social and cultural problem. He feels new generations have lost the tradition of sitting and eating together; lunch breaks have disappeared, locals no longer eat at restaurants and spend most of their time in front of the TV. 'It is deplorable that in a village like this, people are estranged from each other.' His wider cultural critique of contemporary society is reflected in his concerns about the impact of mass tourism and the need to protect Romansch, the local language still used in schools.

He shares with other convivium leaders the view that Slow Food is offering its members more than the mere 'opportunity to eat good food'. His convivium, which meets about five times a year and organises a range of events on wine and cheese tasting, food education, and discussions with local producers, has 40 members in the 45–60 age range, Slow Food's core age group. He sees the role of the convivium as being 'to convince people to change their lifestyles'. 'We live a double life. We try to slow down but at times we have no slow life at all', he tells me. He wants more commitment from his members and stronger public interventions combined with a stronger understanding of the global economic and environmental context. For him 'the critique of globalisation is crucial. It is not enough to just talk of sitting at the table.'

In a very different setting, the Chicago convivium leader Joel Smith, who works as a broker in his day job, was drawn to Slow Food by reasons similar to those outlined by Aerni. It was his empathy with the small producer and the farmers that attracted Smith. 'I cannot appreciate food without making the connection with farmers, the way the food was produced and to support and protect the farmer and the farmland, their product and artisanship and labour required.' In a large convivium of 350 members, Smith organises visits to turkey farms, walking tours to particular parts of the city (notably in areas of ethnic diversity, including Chicago's large Polish community), salt, wine and cheese tastings, a mushroom hunt and food film festival.

One of the biggest initiatives is the city farm in the centre of Chicago. Drawing in youngsters from the rough housing projects, and with the evocative Chicago sky-line behind, the farm produces goods like melons, tomatoes, cucumbers and herbs which are sold to the top restaurants in the city. Smith is inspired by the possibility of changing public attitudes towards food and the range of different issues connected to food. 'Miraculous things happen when you eat real food', he says. He tells me that his co-organiser Janine sees the farmers as the key to change and reminds him that 'we need to make our farmers our new rock stars'.

He also faces some different problems from Aerni in maintaining the commitment of his members; with a rapidly expanding membership a significant problem is how to manage such large numbers, how to keep people involved and continue to address the many different food-related issues. He told me that Slow Food Chicago enjoyed a reasonably high public profile and was 'truly recognised' in the city, but that he was continually 'inundated' with requests from producers, hoteliers and farmers for initiatives.

The expansion of convivia is a problem throughout the US. Erika Lesser, SFUSA's Chief Executive, told me in 2005 that it was the biggest problem she had to deal with. Membership had 'exploded' since the setting up of the national offices in New York in 2000 and they had only just moved to bigger offices in Brooklyn. She told me that the US membership was still mainly made up of professional, affluent members who go to good restaurants, but that the ideas of sustainability and biodiversity had recently recruited a new wave of membership that was more 'politicised'. While California remains the strongest US state, Slow Food is now to be found in all regions and Lesser was pleased to tell me it had broken through in smaller towns. While it retains its biggest numerical strength in the cities – notably New York, San Francisco, Chicago and Los Angeles – it is also making inroads in southern states and rural areas.

The presence of Slow Food in the major cities has enabled it to keep a regular presence and profile amongst opinion formers, as well as being able to call on a growing range of influential public figures. In New York, the Union Square greenmarket is held four days a week, involving 150 producers, including some third generation farmers. Ed Yowell, a recently retired, newly married, convivium leader, tells me that out of the 950 New York members, a third are involved in the food business, while 150 New York restaurants are sourced from farmers' markets in New York state. A convinced food enthusiast, who can quote the eighteenth-century French gastronome, Brillat-Savarin ('Tell me what you eat and I'll tell you what you are'), Yowell says he has a steering committee of nine and the big organisational work is done by a group of 25 members. His passion for food is evident, as he accompanies me around Union Square, and explains his belief that public space needs to be 're-claimed' for more food initiatives as the 'food revolution has to benefit everybody, not just the few'.

It is not surprising that San Francisco, the city most synonymous with the cultural and political movements of the 1960s counter-culture, should provide the heartbeat of Slow Food USA. Because of its strong organic food culture, the availability of quality wines from Sonoma County and a surplus of critically aware consumers, there are more than 3,000 members and 20 convivia in California alone. Yet, there are many paradoxes. It is also the land of the slick movers and shakers of Silicon Valley; state statistics on the industrialisation of agriculture and factory food production are high; and there are high levels of contaminated drinking water. Yet, the growth of Slow Food has been rapid, and proceeded alongside wider shifts in favour of organic agriculture and consumers' organisations.

Within the San Francisco Bay Area alone there are 120 farmers' markets, an increase of 40 per cent since 2000. One of these is the Ferry Plaza Farmers' Market in the centre of San Francisco and at the juncture of one of the busiest transport intersections (ferries, trolley-bus, taxis and trams) in California. This market attracts 15,000–25,000 people on Saturdays and is a popular meeting point for organic food enthusiasts. Jane Connors, the manager of Ferry Plaza marketplace, draws a favourable contrast with the supermarket. 'There is a vibrancy here that you don't get anywhere else. You get the local knowledge that you don't get from the supermarkets.' According to Connors around half the stall-holders (who sell a range of local vegetables, meat and fruit) know of, or have been involved in, Slow Food activities.

I was shown around the market by Carmen Tedesco, co-leader of Slow Food San Francisco convivium, and a self-taught gastronome, who discovered good food while travelling in Europe. One of the events that Tedesco and his colleagues organise here is 'Food From the Heart', at which the stall-holders offer tastings of their products on a candlelit evening in February. Proceeds from the event go towards a local school garden initiative and contribute to funding Terra Madre producers. The convivium also organises a 'Slow Crab Festival', which welcomes the arrival of the Dungeness crab and helps to fund Terra Madre fishermen, as well as a Slow Beer Festival.

Amongst the stall-holders, we heard Rick Knowles, a 30-acre farmer and Slow Food convivium leader from a commuter belt outside San Francisco, explain the problems of getting people, particularly young people, interested in food. It is not a problem at Ferry Plaza, though some say the number of tourists crowd out those who want to cook. Nigel Walker, another farmer, originally from Leicestershire, who brings his produce to Ferry Plaza in a truck run on recycled vegetable oil, agrees that the most important thing is the 'education of the customer'. His own 'Eatwell Farm' offers visits and he has built up a strong network of customers through the Community Supported Agriculture Scheme. According to Walker, the 'farm belongs to the CSA', whose members take produce back regularly in exchange for their membership fee. This provides the security for the farm as well as expanding the support and knowledge network of those committed to organic farming.

The San Francisco convivium's main event is the Golden Glass wine tasting, organised every June by Lorenzo Scarpone, which takes place at Fort Mason, involving small, Italian wine producers and some of the city's best restaurants. San Francisco is a big fund-raising convivium which is able to use the proceeds of its events to support Terra Madre and other initiatives. It is true that the convivium benefits from an affluent membership in a very prosperous city and state. Some have criticised the prices at Ferry Plaza. Carlo Petrini himself, while on one of his many visits to San Francisco, referred to the high prices of produce which caused a prolonged discussion across the organic community websites.

Similar criticisms have been made of some of the Slow Food events in London, which has a similar size convivium to San Francisco (though not the range of events or strength of movement), and which as a result has now capped the entry price to its events at £50. Part of the problem is the cultural assumptions about food and elitism which are shared within British and American cultures, in contrast with Italy and France, with the consequence that the leaders and activists are often labelled in this way. There is of course an 'intellectual challenge', as Silvija Davidson, London Slow Food convivium leader argues, 'to get people to think about what a fair price is' with respect to the work of the producer.

The San Francisco convivium has expanded its network beyond the normal gourmet culture, with its school gardens and educational initiatives. Some of the biggest have been driven by the nearby Chez Panisse Foundation in Berkeley, which, inspired by Alice Waters, has made big inroads into the eating habits of local schools. Set up in 1996, on the twenty-fifth anniversary of the restaurant, the Chez Panisse Foundation 'envisions a school curriculum and school lunch program where growing, cooking and sharing food at the table gives students the knowledge and values to build a humane and sustainable future'. Its 'Edible Schoolyard' at the Martin Luther King Middle School in Berkeley has seen over 3,000 students pass through, while 95 per cent of processed foods have been eliminated from the menus of six district schools. Since 2004, the school lunch programme has made significant improvements in the quality of school dinners in the Berkeley area.[7]

San Francisco, as with other US cities, has also made inroads with regard to the issues of ethnic foods, tackling racism and the use of migrant labour in the food system. Plans for the Slow Food Nation Event in 2008 included space for small ethnic restaurants and 'Fast Slow Food' stalls of Vietnamese cuisine. Amongst the political sessions at the event, there will be major collaborations between social justice organisations, NGOs and Slow Food. The event is to celebrate diversity, according to Anya Fernald, Slow Food Nation organiser, while being 'very political and transformative'. The event is to be organised along familiar Slow Food lines, with the political meetings held in the Civic Centre and the tastings at Fort Mason. Fernald and Alice Waters expected 50,000 people, while leading thinkers such as Michael Pollan, Eric Schlosser, the opera director Peter Sellars, and Vandana Shiva are to be keynote speakers.

The possibility of engaging with the diverse cultural traditions of a big city – something beyond small, provincial towns like Bra – has been apparent in many cities in the US. It has also been part of the London agenda. Zeenat Anjari, of the environmental group *Sustain*, rejects the claim that Slow Food appeals to an elite minority or that it cannot engage with or explain how ethnic foods fit into its political and cultural agendas. Part of her role with *Sustain* has included working with ethnic minority producers and restaurants through the London Food Link, providing advice on sustainability and using local produce. In fact, her experiences suggest that many ethnic dishes can be sourced locally, according to seasonality, and that this practice is already well established amongst minority ethnic businesses and restaurants, with food often sourced from existing local supply chains *within* communities. One of many examples she cites is the Rastafarian Stoshus restaurant in Hackney, in an area enriched by local markets. Anjari, brought up in Britain, from an East-African Asian family, also dismisses the association between food, pleasure and elitism as 'Western guilt', which betrays a failure to recognise the status that food carries in all cultures, and the pleasures it delivers within all communities. Her experience of working with Slow Food provided an interesting contrast with government bodies. Slow Food, she argued, talked of 'sensuality, emotion, identity and place', while government jargon rarely got beyond targets and outcomes.

The number of farmers' markets, the links with community-supported agriculture (CSAs), city farms and other projects, provide more scope for convivia leaders to act out their role as gastronomes in the way envisaged by Petrini. The strength of Slow Food lies in its ability to penetrate very different cultures and environments. The gastronomes who organise its activities are also a varied mix. In Sicily, Rosario Gugliotta, convivium leader ('*fiduciario*' in Italian) of Messina Valdelmone, who works for a pharmaceutical company by day, organises a phenomenal range of activities on the island. He admitted, as he drove me through the vast spaces of the Parco Nebrodi, that Slow Food was his 'passion'. Gugliotta himself has developed a wide knowledge of food and knows producers all over Sicily, including the group which breed the 'suino nero' (black pig), in a part of the Nebrodi mountains accessible only by 4×4 vehicles. This unique breed, found in the beech and oak forests, is a Slow Food Presidia product and deemed under threat. The response is to promote the local salami, sausage and *prosciutto*. The Parco Nebrodi itself is a land of rich vegetation and wildlife in the largest protected area in Sicily. Gugliotta helps to organise educational visits to the area and has collaborated with the park over Slow Food events.

Our next stop was the small town of Nizza near Messina, where Gugliotta introduces me to Attilio Interdonato, whose family has been producing the Interdonato lemons since the last century, when his great-grandfather Giovanni Interdonato, an officer in Garibaldi's army, first crossed a citron with ariddaru, a local variety of lemon. This product, which had been popular in the UK in the post-war period, underwent a crisis in the 1980s, and was now being revived by Slow Food through its Presidia scheme. Speaking to me with the vast family home an evocative image in the hills behind, Attilio Interdonato is clearly proud of the heritage of his lemons, and sees the intervention of Slow Food as crucial to its survival.

Amongst the events Gugliotta organises is 'Salina Slow', an annual four-day event on the Aeolian Island of between two and three thousand inhabitants (made famous by Michael Radford's film *Il Postino*). This event, on an island which is less tourist-centred than its more affluent neighbour Lipari, celebrates the two local Presidia products, capers and Malvasia, a sweet dessert wine. Salina Slow is organised through collaboration between local restaurants, hotels and producers, while those attending are given tours, tastings and the opportunity to spend time with local people. Most tourists go on day trips; Salina Slow embodies the Slow Food ideal of tourists as temporary residents or guests.

One of the organisers of Salina Slow is Aldo Bacciulli, the Catania convivium leader and chef-owner of the acclaimed Metro restaurant in the historic centre of Sicily's second city. Bacciulli belongs to the original Slow Food generation, was a member of Arcigola and displays the Slow Food Manifesto alongside the menu. He has a wide knowledge of local food and gives me a guided tour of Catania fish market, where traders barter and cajole each other in Sicilian dialect. In Sicily, Slow Food has a growing presence with 300 members in the Messina convivium, and 200 each in Catania, Palermo and Siracusa. It represents an important part of the 'other story' of associationism and civic activism in a land so often thwarted by the mafia, unemployment and fatalism.

In Oslo, the epitome of an environmentally progressive, modern and enlightened city, Marit Mogstad, an organisa-tional psychologist by day, who also contributes to women's magazines and a local radio station, organises a convivium of around 100 members, made up of 40-plus 'Italophiles'. Slow Food is her 'hobby', and she describes her convivium membership as composed of 'informed consumers' with a particular 'love for Italy'. She has around ten core activists and, as with other convivium leaders, is under pressure to organise the range of activities and keep the members involved.

In one of the world's most expensive cities for food and drink, the difficulty is getting younger members with families involved, while the links with the producers are not as strong as elsewhere in Norway, such as the fishing communities in the north west of the country. Consequently, the events include dinners celebrating seasonal food, including local asparagus, and tasting of Chablis and speciality beers. Links with local restaurants are limited to the local Spiseforretning, whose chef Jarle Baer is a Slow Food sympathiser.

Slow Food convivium leaders have a range of backgrounds and perform multiple roles whether as organisers, educators or mediators. The extent to which they have realised the identity of 'co-producers' has been partly determined by the very different economic and local circumstances in which they find themselves. The *political* urgency of their work is also dependent on local situations. In Eastern Europe, according to Jacek Szklarek, convivium leader of Krakow, most of the work is concerned with producers and is less consumer-focused, with the priority given to enabling small producers to develop their businesses. This is even more striking in developing countries. In Kenya, for example, the Slow Food Central Rift convivium, one of six Kenya convivia, focuses on building partnerships with small producers, chefs and school gardens projects, in adverse economic conditions. This work was thrown into crisis at the beginning of 2008, following the Kenyan election and the onset of ethnic violence. The convivium became part of the support network in helping resettlement of the thousands of people fleeing the violence.

Slow Food convivium leaders have assumed an unlikely but important 'political' role in their attachment to food, and their ability to articulate a critical global and environmental awareness. Along with the producers, they have become important new political subjects in the new territory of politics and pleasure.

5

The Return of the Producer ...
and the Death of the Consumer?

THE RISE OF THE critical or ethical consumer has been one of the most significant developments in politics in recent years. In an age widely regarded as one of political disengagement, whereby citizens have become apathetic, isolated from the political process and alienated from the values of citizenship, the rise of the critical consumer has been the exception to the rule. Ranging from environmental campaigns to boycotts and alternative purchasing, these new consumers have exercised an increasingly powerful political voice. Ethical and critical consumption has often challenged the moral basis of contemporary capitalism, in respect of fair trade or environmental sustainability, and has stimulated innovative forms of political engagement. Different strategies have sought to withdraw from 'mass' consumption (boycotting of supermarkets, for example) or encouraged alternative forms of consumption, for example, purchasing environmentally friendly or organic produce. This greater awareness and public attention has made shopping a more political activity in that consumers often express more informed views about the origins of produce and the practices of retailers. These new forms of political participation, in which the construction of new political identities has become evident, as well as the articulation of different lifestyles, have informed and questioned the basis of contemporary society.

These developments have begun to have profound implications. Companies have had to respond to new pressures on safety and the environment, forcing them into new commitments and statements on 'corporate social responsibility', while supermarkets have increasingly had to justify to their customers that they have at least some commitment to the environment or fair trade, and increasingly compete against each other to prove their environmental credentials. Despite the response of companies and the greater public awareness, the bigger political questions of global economics and social justice remain highly contested. Nevertheless, these consumers can be described as new political actors, able to influence public debate, through 'symbolic campaigns', networks and protests.

In the area of food, the critical consumer has demanded sustainable practices in the production of food, including an increase in organic produce, justice for small farmers in developing countries, humane treatment of animals, opposition to genetically modified food, greater food safety, reduction in shopping miles and support for local produce. There has been a significant expansion of networks on sustainability and the promotion of local food, with the result that there has been more interest and empathy for the producer. Slow Food activists have been part of many of these developments. These include support, at a local convivium level, for organic food, for promoting local produce and for a critical approach – made clear in meetings, discussions and publications – towards standardised goods which have travelled many miles. The promotion of local goods in fairs and farmers' markets, tastings of local produce, and educational initiatives which raise awareness about food, are the main type of Slow Food activities which could be described as alternative consumption.

While Slow Food's international sections such as the Slow Food Foundation for Biodiversity and events such as Slow Fish and Terra Madre have organised a range of initiatives, often in collaboration with other NGOs and movements such as Fair Trade, Slow Food has normally avoided boycotts and campaigns against supermarkets or fast food stores, preferring to focus on developing links with small producers and alternative forms of economic and social development. As Rainer Riedi, leader of the Bundner Herrshaft convivium in Switzerland, told me: Slow Food is 'not only a movement against, but [also about] how things can be in the future'. For Riedi, a long-standing Greenpeace member, this was a distinctive difference between Slow Food and other movements. Some exceptions to this were the 'No GM Wine' campaign Slow Food launched in 2000 against the 'commercialisation of transgenic vines', as well as local oppositions to supermarket or fast food expansions that Slow Food activists have taken part in. Normally, the Slow Food position is to defend and protect artisan products at risk of extinction rather than to openly challenge or confront major corporations.

Therefore, while Slow Food can be seen as part of the alternative consumption movement, there are some significant differences. One is the holistic critique Slow Food has made of the global economic system, emphasising the links between third world poverty and the failure of sustainable development or investment in local producers. Second, Slow Food's empathy lies essentially with the producer, a relationship which has been strengthened since the arrival of Terra Madre. It is not solely a consumer movement which acts on behalf of, or merely in alliance with, producers. Rather it is a movement which is committed to the liberation of the producer, to resituating the centrality of traditional producers, drawing on their local knowledge and artisan skills. This is reflected in the description of the enlightened consumer as a 'co-producer' and by the emphasis on 'food communities', in which consumers and producers are brought together and benefit from mutual exchange.

Slow Food's appeal, then, is for critical consumers to take a further step, to overcome the widening divisions between producer and consumer, indeed to go beyond 'consumerism'. Only then would we be able to 'eat responsibly', in the words of Wendell Berry, one of the thinkers most admired by Carlo Petrini.

> Eating is an agricultural act. ... Most eaters, however, are no longer aware that this is true. They think of food as an agricultural product, perhaps, but they do not think of themselves as participants in agriculture. They think of themselves as 'consumers'. If they think beyond that, they recognise that they are passive consumers.[1]

According to Berry, most people ignore the key issues concerning not only the quality and cost of food, including how fresh the produce is, how it was transported, the cost of marketing and packaging, but also, crucially, the type of farms and the knowledge and skills needed to produce it: 'the industrial eater is, in fact, one who does not know that eating is an agricultural act, who no longer knows or imagines the connection between eating and the land, and who is therefore necessarily passive and uncritical – in short, a victim'.[2] Berry regards the position of the 'passive consumer' as one amounting to alienation, which impinges on their freedom to live freely and responsibly.

> Our kitchens and other eating places more and more resemble filling stations, as our homes more and more resemble motels ... The passive American consumer sitting down to a meal of pre-prepared or fast food, confronts a platter covered with inert, anonymous substances that have been processed, dyed, breaded, sauced, gravied, ground, pulped, strained, blended, prettified and sanitized beyond resemblance to any part of any creature that ever lived. ... Eaters ... must understand that eating takes place inescapably in the world, that it is inescapably an agricultural act, and that how we eat determines, to a considerable extent, how the world is used.[3]

For Berry, this lack of awareness has assumed democratic significance and he urges consumers to participate more in the production of food, by growing their own produce where they can, preparing their own food, knowing more about the origins of food, buying directly from local farmers and small producers, getting to know more about industrial farming and its alternatives, and learning about the variety of food species. Berry was writing in 1988, but his analysis fits closely with the development of Slow Food's position, and his recommendations are similar to the arguments made by Slow Food activists. His call for greater understanding of the way food is produced is close to Slow Food's view that we should no longer talk of consumers, but of 'co-producers', a term which they apply to their own members in the various convivia. Carlo Petrini has equated what he sees as the ever widening gap between consumption and production with the cutting of an 'umbilical cord' that had previously been

> guaranteed by the proximity between agricultural practice, processing, and consumption ... we must change our attitudes, starting with our terminology. *Consuming* is the final act of the production process: it should be seen as such, and not as extraneous to the process. The old consumer must therefore begin to feel in some way part of the production process – getting to know it, influencing it with his preferences, supporting it if it is in difficulty, rejecting it if it is wrong or unsustainable. The old consumer, now the new *gastronome*, must begin to feel like a *co-producer* [his emphasis].[4]

This recentring of the producer informs Slow Food's analysis of the 'fast life', the impact of industrial agriculture, standardised produce and the plight of small producers. It also echoes earlier nineteenth-century fears about the erosion of the skills and artisanship of craft workers, the commitment to preserving the 'dignity' of the producer and the impact of 'technique' over wisdom and knowledge. The work of William Morris is important in this respect. The life and work of this English

Marxist – who was first drawn to socialism in the mid nineteenth century, when industrial capitalism was emerging triumphant as the new economic order, which led to the loss of important artisan skills – has some important parallels with the predicaments of the producer in the contemporary world of global capitalism.

For Morris, industrial capitalism brought with it not only inequality but also a new philistinism, symbolised by a new squalor and vulgarity. As an admirer of the pre-Raphaelites while a student at Oxford, Morris was initially drawn to the romantic world of art and literature in defiance of the domination of money and profit. John Keats, Blake and other poets and writers had expressed a commitment to the 'passions' of the artist, and the need to free man's sensory values and humanity from the corruptions of industrial capitalist society. His defence of architecture in opposition to attempts to restore old buildings was influenced by John Ruskin's *The Nature of Gothic*, which praised the craftsmanship of the original gothic buildings. For Morris this respect for the skills of craftsman, for the beauty of art and the threat to these values from industrial capitalism, became increasing concerns. His work has many similarities with the contemporary concerns of Slow Food, notably in his empathy for the producer and the questioning of the division between manual and mental labour, his recognition of art, his uncompromising attitudes towards aesthetic pleasure and, as his thought progressed, the development of his critique of a way of living.

For Morris, in 1877, the competition generated by industrial capitalism had led to 'sham' workmanship, 'hurtful to the buyer, more hurtful to the seller, if only he knew it, most hurtful to the maker...'. The public was now offered, in this emerging plutocracy where wealth had come to power, 'cheap goods' and 'nasty wares', over excellence and beauty. 'England has of late', Morris told an audience in Oxford Street, London, 'been too much busied with the counting-house and not enough with the workshop.'[5]

Morris' crusade is in some ways similar to Carlo Petrini's in the recent era. He was thought to have spoken at some 578 meetings between 1883 and 1896, more prodigious even than Petrini, and he shared the Piedmontese's passion as a visionary at odds with contemporary currents, driven by the urgency of intervening, organising and elucidating the society of the future. Morris, himself a talented artist and poet, like Petrini the gastronome with a taste for aesthetic perfection, was deeply embedded in the alternative culture of change. 'Art is long and life is short; let us at least do something before we die', Morris argued. Petrini uses a Piedmontese expression to make the same point, that the world can be made a better place, 'during these four days that are granted to us on this earth' – '*si quatr di che ruma da vivi*'.

The very nature of the plutocratic society described by Morris meant that the skills of the craftsmen were being forgotten. 'Useful work' had been replaced by 'useless toil', characteristic of social inequality and barbarism: 'for if pleasure in labour be generally possible, what a strange folly it must be for men to consent to labour without pleasure; and what a hideous injustice it must be for society to compel most men to labour without pleasure'.[6]

Morris therefore pointed to a major distinction between work that was carried out in industrial society – a type he described as 'toil', a burden on the workers, who created a product that was unnecessary, ugly and cheap – and useful work. This was work that consisted of pleasure in the process of production and in the quality of the product:

> ... a man at work, making something which he feels will exist because he is working at it and wills it, is exercising the energies of his mind and soul as well as of his body. Memory and imagination help him as he works. Not only his own thoughts, but the thoughts of the men of past ages guide his hands; and, as a part of the human

race, he creates. If we work thus we shall be men, and our days will be happy and eventful.[7]

Three aspects are important to keep in mind when considering Morris' view of work with regard to Slow Food. First, his views on useful labour and defending the skills of the craftsmen were shaped primarily by his belief that the skills of artisans were fundamental to the simple pleasures of life. 'Art', he argued, 'is man's expression of his joy in labour.' Second, he had a systemic critique of contemporary society which contrasted the waste, cheapness and ugliness of industrial society with the purity of clean air, man's relationship with nature, and the use of work as a way of fulfilling the simple pleasures of life from which all should benefit. Morris was condemnatory of 'luxury', by which he meant the exclusive privileges afforded to the few at the expense of the many; luxury was the 'sworn foe of pleasure', he argued, because in the race to provide excess of goods for the rich it spoilt natural beauty, and replaced the simple pleasures of life with ugliness and waste. 'Shall I tell you what luxury has done for you in modern Europe?', he asked the Hammersmith branch of the Socialist League, on the evening of 13 November 1887:

It has covered the merry green fields with the hovels of slaves, and blighted the flowers and trees with poisonous gases, and turned the rivers into sewers; till over many parts of Britain the common people have forgotten what a field or a flower is like, and their idea of beauty is a gas-poisoned gin-palace or a tawdry theatre.[8]

There are some striking similarities here too between Morris' emphasis on luxury and Petrini's discussion of 'abundance'. For Petrini, abundance, or 'abbondanza' in Italian, had been given a meaning that was associated with waste and excess, 'taking and taking without questioning what remains for the earth'. Yet, according to Petrini, abundance primarily means 'generosity':

It's a concept that must be considered in terms of sustainability; let's not make a mistake by asking for more. We don't want more food when there is already enough for everyone in the world. ... We don't want to become wealthier in goods or in money; we want everyone to have enough to live properly. Abundance, is therefore, a concept that is also dependent on solidarity. The objective of abundance is widespread well-being.[9]

Third, the centrality of the producer challenges the rigid distinction between mental and manual labour out of respect for the knowledge and creative and artistic talents of craftsmen; skills that plutocratic industrial societies, like technocratic post-industrial societies a century and a half later, were destroying. In this respect, Morris is close to Slow Food because he respects the autonomy of the producers and sees their creative talents as the driving force of an alternative society; they were experts in their own right.

The 'remedy' therefore, according to Morris, 'lies with the handicraftsmen ... the duty and honour of educating the public lies with them'.[10] This is also Slow Food's remedy, which sees the future in the hands of the small producers, those 'intellectuals of the earth', 'who continue to work for their own food freedom and for a clean agriculture that respects social justice'.[11]

This might explain why Slow Food can claim to have gone beyond the description of being a 'consumer movement'. Indeed it transcends the alternative-consumer position because its food communities were to be based around small producers in their locality. The experience of Terra Madre was crucial in this respect because it embedded the work and priorities of Slow Food in the traditions, knowledge and experiences of the producers. This had major implications for the development of Slow Food as a movement, particularly in the way that it involved the developing countries. The growth of Slow Food in developing countries owes much to Terra Madre which, in many cases, formed the basis for the growth of local convivia. The food communities, defined by Slow Food as all the people who work in the 'quality' and 'sustainable' food and agricultural sector with strong connections to their region, were instrumental in establishing Slow Food in many poorer countries. Following a big campaign at Terra Madre in 2006, 555 new Slow Food members were found from the food communities.

In Eastern Europe, the development of Slow Food was also driven by the experiences and economic needs of small producers. In the Saxon village of Transylvania in Romania – which suffered from major emigration following the end of communism (with up to 90 per cent of villagers moving to Germany), and a continuing economic crisis in the subsequent years – Slow Food worked with the Adept Foundation to support local producers find markets for their products. Romania was a country of 4 million people heavily dependent on agriculture, that was threatened by depopulation, the intensification of industrial agriculture and global economic pressure. The Saxon villages – which were in an area of outstanding natural beauty and biodiversity, recognised by the award of UNESCO World Heritage status in 1999 – were used to producing for home consumption, and had little experience of producing for wider markets.

Local people had produced plum schnapps, goats cheese and jams for years, but in a country with little historical memory of small private businesses, there were many obstacles to overcome in helping producers get off the ground. In addition, following Romania's entry to the EU, European legislation was not favourable. As Anca Calagar of Adept told me, the producers were frustrated by the EU rules. 'They cannot market their wine, because they have to pay huge taxes and they don't have financial power. It is shocking for them that someone can tell you: "no it is not possible to do that anymore".' More worrying were the EU safety laws which had major implications for cheese production amongst other things. During the time of

my visit, a major training programme for small inexperienced
producers was under way, so that appropriate levels of food
hygiene were met, including adequate size kitchens, special
sinks and other facilities. For cheese producers this included
dealing with problems of pasteurisation and of contamination
from milk. According to Ben Mehudin, an Adept Co-ordinator,
before it 'was almost impossible for ordinary people to have
facilities like these'. In the state farms safety standards had
been good, but the products had been tasteless, while industrialised farming under the communist system threatened the
natural resources.

In the case of jam production, the question was how these
sustainable wild fruit preserves of exceptional value could
be marketed. Without a market, and with a declining Saxon
culture, this particular tradition of jam-making, based on ancient
recipes and the quality of the local fruits, was under threat. In
2005 Slow Food, in collaboration with Adept, sent a team of
experts to taste the jams and assess their quality, production
methods and traditions. They found not only quality (derived
partly from the greater balance of fruit to sugar), but also that
an activity which had been carried out for many years was
central to the culture and local environment. By providing the
Saxon Village Preserves with Presidia status, Slow Food brought
together different producers and enabled them to market their
products. The producers themselves also recognised the role
of Slow Food in changing their circumstances.

One of the jam producers was Gerda Gherghiceanu.
A resident of Viscri, a typical Saxon village, with no cars,
exceptional wildlife, and where the rituals of animal husbandry
continue, she went to Terra Madre in 2006, sold lots of jams
and did many TV interviews. Terra Madre also made her aware
of wider issues such as the plight of Africa, and gave her the
chance to exchange ideas with jam producers in other countries.
Both Gerda and the other producers felt that the development
of their produce for sale in the market was helping to preserve

the identity of their villages, whose culture was threatened, as well as keeping important knowledge and tradition alive.

In Romania, the initial development of Slow Food was inextricably linked to work with the producers, and the subsequent development of the movement there has been shaped by their activities. Gerda's son Cristi has been the main link between Slow Food and the small producers of the region. He sees the work with the local producers as crucial to the development of the wider Transylvania region, which has suffered from depopulation and is threatened by the intensification of agriculture. Yet there is unworked land of rich, natural resources which still needs investment; 'conservation without money is conversation', Cristi argues.

The success of the jam producers had a positive effect on the development of Slow Food in Romania. At the first public event of the new Bucharest convivium, at the Bucharest film festival in 2007, their products were on sale along with other local Romanian produce, while Romania's first farmers' market was established later the same year with the help of the producers and Slow Food.

In Poland, the growth of Slow Food was also initially driven by the producers and sustained through producer-based convivia. In the summer of 2000, Piero Sardo, then working with the Slow Food Presidia, visited the Tatra mountain region to speak to the shepherds who produced Oscypek cheese, a smoked, hard sheep's milk cheese made since the fourteenth century and normally served with vodka or beer. Sardo was impressed with the taste and the methods of production and after the usual evaluation procedures it became a Presidia product.

This meeting, and the subsequent visit of the shepherds to the Salone del Gusto in Turin in 2002, was the catalyst for the development of Slow Food in Poland. At the time of the visit to the Salone, Polish law did not allow the export of the cheese for commercial purposes so they smuggled the product in bags under bus seats on their journey. Most of the cheese was sold out following mass queues on the first day of the Salone, and it received a lot of coverage on the Italian media. For the shepherds themselves the experience was a life-changing one, visiting the sea for the first time in their lives and receiving a lot of attention; another example, after years of neglect and repression, of the restored dignity of the producer in Eastern Europe.

Jacek Szklarek, who was the first initial Slow Food contact in Poland (and who had discovered Slow Food while a student in Italy), became the Presidium co-ordinator and the organiser of the main Slow Food events in Poland. He told me that much of the work of the five Polish convivia, in Warsaw and Krakow, was centred on the producers. The second Polish Presidia product was the mead produced by Maciej Jaros, from his house just outside Warsaw. This product, made from honey, matures for six to seven years. He sells it in ceramic containers and, as he shows me around his production site, pointing out the hives in remote locations, he has an obvious pride in his work. He has been producing mead for 15 years and learned the trade from his grandmother. Under communism, mead was presented as a gift for Polish Ministers and important officials but remained an unfashionable drink (he quips that communist leaders thought the people would be calmer without mead and less likely to protest). After the system collapsed there was a lack of quality mead available, and Maciej had the foresight to buy the registered mead company when the government lifted the ban on small businesses in 1991. He has a shop as well as the workshop on site (he also breeds horses) and tells me of the 'spiritual' capacities of mead to bring good health. He has pride in this artisan product which goes back centuries, and with the help of Slow Food, has sought to ensure mead is sold at a fair price – not an easy task in reviving an old product that lost popularity, while there were also many cheaper, inferior products on the market. According to Szklarek, the granting of Presidia status to mead has had a 'huge effect' and led to greater press and publicity, ensuring that 'Poles are now discussing mead'.

In addition to improving the marketing of the product, Maciej's experience, as is the case with other Slow Food producers, has contributed to wider projects launched by Slow Food. This included a major initiative launched in Poland on sustainable agriculture, biodiversity and tackling global poverty, supported by the European Union and opened by Poland's Ministry of Agriculture in September 2007. Maciej was one of the speakers at the opening event, which brought together Slow Food, Fair Trade representatives and producers.

Other examples of Eastern European products benefiting from the input of Slow Food include the Mangalica sausage in Hungary, a sweet cured sausage derived from an ancient breed of pig, distinguished by its rich and curly coat, and produced by eleven pig farmers who work together on organic and co-operative farms, south of Budapest. In Bosnia-Herzegovina and Armenia, Slow Food has worked with plum preserve and apricot producers in poor countries ravaged by war, where producers have struggled to survive. Since 2000 Slow Food has had a growing presence in Belarus, where it has held a Terra Madre event as well as supporting producers in a range of initiatives. All these countries have connections to the land but are also places without a history of tourism.

In Eastern Europe, the producers have therefore had many battles to contend with, including EU legislation which has often presented many obstacles to developing their products, and trying to rebuild a lost gastronomic culture in circumstances very different from Western Europe has been an arduous process. Despite the fact that the recent history of Eastern Europe has left people suspicious of ideology and reluctant to join associations, with civil society still being remade in parts of Eastern Europe, Slow Food has played a part in this development. It has had to work hard to break down these negative perceptions, a process made easier, according to

Lilia Smelkova, Slow Food co-ordinator of Eastern European countries, by Terra Madre.

The relationship between producers and ordinary Slow Food members has been different in the West, because of the different history and origins of Slow Food here. In the UK, for example, where the links between Slow Food and producers have not been notably strong, much of Slow Food's work with producers has been through the rise of farmers' markets. In 1997 there were no farmers' markets in the UK but by 2008 there were over 500, bringing in £1.1 billion a year for 46,000 traders manning 150,000 stalls.[12] Over half of these have received certification from FARMA, the National Farmers' Retail and Markets Association. Slow Food has established relationships with the producers at these markets in different parts of the country, though, according to convivium leaders, there is a varying depth of Slow Food identity amongst the producers. In London there are 14 markets which cover most parts of the city, including thriving ones in less affluent areas like Peckham and Walthamstow.

In the US there is also a mixed picture between those convivia which consist mainly of ordinary members and those which have developed close links with producers. There are many examples of these, thanks to the degree of commitment and activity, the spiralling of organic food and sustainable agriculture initiatives, notably the community-supported agriculture schemes. These are strongest in California and New York but they have a presence in all parts of the US. As Deena Goldman of the Slow Food USA office told me, there has been a 'quiet revolution' taking place in states like Ohio, Iowa and Wisconsin, 'where the food of this country is grown and where people hear and feel the effects of an industrialised food system the most'. This revolution is driven by farmers who have decided to look for alternatives to industrial farming.

At Fountain Prairie Farm, deep in the hills of Wisconsin, just beyond the Fall River off Highway 16, John and Dorothy

Priske, two middle-aged farmers, talk about the revolution they believe in. 'Some years ago,' John tells me, 'we decided that we weren't happy with the way farming was going.' The main problem was with 'industrialised agriculture', which, through its over-dependence on chemicals, was preventing the development of socially responsible and environmentally sound farming.

It was a visit to New Zealand in 2000 that proved to be the turning-point for the Priskes. There, they admired the flavour of the lamb they were served and discovered it had been raised solely on grass. That same year, another event made them rethink further the quality of their lives when their two dogs died from different forms of cancer. It occurred to them that their industrialised farming techniques, notably the overuse of chemicals, may have contributed to the deaths.

These two events led to what Dorothy calls their 'epiphany', and they started over. By the end of the year, they had switched to a 'natural' grass-based system, using no hormones, anabolic steroids or feed antibiotics. The only question now was: which animals would be best suited to do the harvesting and fertilising? In February 2001, the first twelve Scottish Highland cattle arrived at the farm. This shaggy, red-haired, award-winning heritage breed was chosen because it didn't need shelter in the winter and had the capacity to cope with lesser quality forage. Above all, the flavour of the meat is of the highest quality. Following their arrival, the cattle were raised in a humane manner, while the farm itself became totally organic and committed to biodiversity.

This change has not made the Priskes rich, but it has left them culturally fulfilled. In 2003, they transformed their farm into a bed and breakfast, with the cattle the star attraction for guests, while they are now able to serve freshly made organic produce in a beautifully restored nineteenth-century farmhouse. They have a regular stall at the Dane County farmers' market, one of the biggest in the US, and are justly proud of the quality of their cattle. More importantly, the change in their own circumstances has involved them in a wider battle which they consider vital to the future of agriculture as well as central to the quality of life in the US.

It may be premature to announce the death of the consumer, but Slow Food's concept of the 'co-producer' has raised important issues about the meaning of contemporary consumption. Petrini himself has suggested that the role of the consumer, which has become so distant from the work of the producer, needs to be redefined. Consuming, he argues, is the 'final act' of the production process and it needs to be recognised as part of it, rather than, as too often at present, cut off and indifferent to it. By focusing on the producer Slow Food has raised questions about the condition of the local economy and gone beyond mere protest to consider how alternative economic relationships can be realised between producer and consumer at a local level. It is believed that aligning consumers and producers will bring their interests closer and foster more interdependency. It is the task of Slow Food, which is both a network and a movement, to transcend the differences between consumer and producer and unite them in what Petrini calls 'a community of destiny'.[13]

6

The Movement

SLOW FOOD'S MEMBERSHIP of 84,000 people in over 120 different countries belies a very complex and differentiated membership structure. As a movement born in Italy, whose own membership at the end of 2007 was nearly half that of the movement as a whole, the development of Slow Food is dependent on it appealing beyond its country of origin. This is not an easy proposition. Italy has over 400 convivia and 195 of the 300 Presidia products are Italian. With Slow Food's offices based in Bra (where it is the second largest employer in the town), the majority of its Presidia and events organised in Italy, and its evolution and political culture reflecting an Italian strain, moving beyond Italy was always going to be one of Slow Food's biggest challenges.

It was not just the numerical strength that has made Slow Food an Italian movement. Slow Food has created and sustained a strong public presence in Italy. Its *Osterie d'Italia*, the guide to quality eating places, has sold in excess of 100,000 copies annually since it was founded in 1991, and to be listed as one of its chosen establishments is a coveted reward sought by owners of trattorias and osterias throughout Italy. Teams of experts, normally Slow Food employees, are sent out to judge, following strict criteria of quality, based on taste, use of local seasonal products, and cost. The history of an osteria is also important in the descriptions that appear in the guide, as is the architecture and the conviviality of the surroundings, but it is the quality of food which is the defining factor. Restaurants awarded accreditation display the Slow Food snail sign in the window, though this is no guarantee they will be entered the following year. The *Osterie* guide holds an annual awards celebration in October, with a different venue every year. The Slow Food Editore which publishes the *Osterie d'Italia* also produces a range of other books on wine, recipes and food history. It also occupies an important place at Slow Food events such as the Salone del Gusto, Slow Fish, held every two years in Genoa, and Cheese, the biennial cheese show in Bra, with discussions, book launches and informal gatherings of writers and journalists.

The Slow Food Editore is one of several ways through which Slow Food has established a regular public space. The Slow Food events themselves offer spaces for meetings, press events and book signings as well as tastings. Carlo Petrini has an expanding public profile, writing regularly for *La Repubblica* and other national newspapers and is on first-name terms with leading politicians and broadcasters. The Slow Food press office has five full-time staff and with its growing range of contacts in Italy can get regular news stories into the press.

The 'Italian' nature of Slow Food therefore cannot be under-estimated. As we have seen, in its origins the development of Slow Food has owed much to Carlo Petrini's role as a political and cultural entrepreneur. As someone who understood cultural politics and had a close identification with the territory of the Langhe, Petrini has been able to draw on his local experiences as he has shaped the direction of the movement. His earlier involvement with the *Cantè i'euv* and Radio Bra Red Waves helped provide the political and cultural foundations of Slow Food, while his knowledge of the local food and wine traditions, including his extensive engagement with those who worked in food and wine production, gave him more than a conventional political insight. This was a form of cultural politics which had its origins in the quasi-anarchic but creative moment of left politics in the 1970s where there was an optimism that it was possible to change the world through a political engagement with popular culture.

But the Italian origins of Slow Food have also influenced the regional focus so crucial to Slow Food's identity. Petrini and his contemporaries the 'first generation' of Slow Food leaders – brought with them a particular way of working and a political culture which has influenced the dynamics of the organisation. Petrini's own great merit is as an organiser and as somebody who can spot talent and bring people into the organisation, along with a capacity for raising the public profile of the movement. Many of his senior colleagues originated from Bra, or were in similar political organisations in the wider Langhe area. In addition to Azio Citi and the late Giovanni Ravinale, these included Piero Sardo, whose three sons, Renato, Sebastiano and Stefano have all held prominent positions in Slow Food; Silvio Barbero, a former CGIL organiser; Gigi Piumatti, a wine expert; and Marcello Marengo, who has become Slow Food's resident photographer. Giulio Colomba, a former communist mayor from Friuli-Venezia Giulia, has also been involved from the start. Most of these continue to work for Slow Food, in various ways, either as employees or as volunteers, and still have the ear of Petrini. Younger members of this group include Paola Nano, a long-standing member of the press office and a former comrade of Petrini's in the PDUP, and Cinzia Scaffidi, born into a Sicilian family but living in Bra, who was recruited by Petrini while she was editor of the local communist youth paper.

Since Slow Food established its international office in the early 1990s, another generation of mainly 'Braidese' organisers and activists have emerged, most of whom are now in their early to mid thirties. Many were spotted by Petrini through their local involvement, though, unlike the first generation, most of them do not have the same allegiance to left-wing political organisations. This generation includes Paolo

Di Croce, the head of the international office, Alessandro Monchiero of the Communications Office, Olivia Reviglio, Laura Bonino, who works in Petrini's office, Roberto Burdese, President of Slow Food Italy, Serena Milano, co-ordinator of the Slow Food Foundation, and Carlo Bogliotti, who helps Petrini with his journalism and writing and is an influential figure in the background.

Indeed, the circumstances in which Bogliotti first got involved with Slow Food nicely illuminates Petrini's style and his distinctive knack of finding and involving people in Slow Food's projects. Bogliotti, while a journalist student at Turin University, worked as a volunteer 'nightwatchman' at the first edition of the Cheese event in Bra in 1997, safeguarding the cheese and wine on display in the big marquee. On the last night, Petrini, along with Azio Citi and others, joined him and, in a party atmosphere (asking jokingly if Bogliotti had stolen any of the cheese), gave Bogliotti an impromptu wine and cheese tasting test. Within six months Bogliotti was working on the organisation of the second Salone del Gusto in 1998. By 2001 he was working in the president's office and has become a regular confidant of Petrini. He has subsequently been present at the beginning of each new Slow Food project from the University of Gastronomic Sciences to Terra Madre. Petrini's habit was to call him at night and say 'I have an idea' and arrange to meet the next morning. These informal discussions with Petrini take place in Piedmontese dialect and are invariably the prelude to subsequent formal meetings as the projects evolve. According to Bogliotti, Petrini was particularly skilled at spotting young people and bringing them into the organisation. He describes the Slow Food office in Bra as one based on human relationships where people have a similar background and share like-minded beliefs, cultivated and orchestrated by Petrini's creativity and genius. The international offices have subsequently been the place where leading members of national organisations are brought into the organisation, given training and introduced to the language and culture of the Slow Food movement. There are now around 150 members working in the seven offices in Bra. They are paid between 1,100 and 1,900 euros a month and, as with other movements, expected to work long hours and make reasonable sacrifices for the cause.[1] Perhaps unsurprisingly, according to some of those who work there, 'slow' principles are not always prominent in the working practices of the institution: as with other movements, the rush to get press releases translated and to meet deadlines creates its own pressures. But it seems free, too, of the managerialism of mainstream organisations, while retaining its own originality and independence. Anya Fernald, who worked in the Slow Food offices for four years before returning home to California to work for CAFF (Community Alliance with Family Farmers), says she misses the 'craziness' of Slow Food. 'Every day we had a new fantasy.' She thought the office was an interesting mix of local people looking for work and those with a strong political commitment to the cause. As Slow Food expands and draws in committed activists from outside the small Piedmont town of less than 25,000 people, it is not surprising that some outsiders (including from other parts of Italy) sometimes feel a bit left out of the Bra story.

The Italian context, driven by the local knowledge of the Braidese, remains pivotal therefore in the development of Slow Food. However, the Italian influence has extended beyond Italy and has been important in the development of several national Slow Food associations. This has been significant through the personal contacts between Petrini and particular members of Slow Food, as well as at a more general cultural level. In some cases leaders of national associations, like Otto Geisel of Germany, have become involved after a personal encounter with Petrini. Geisel met him at a Bordeaux wine fair in 1992, when he found him sitting at his own small table, attempting to attract people to Arcigola. He and Geisel had dinner together that night deep in the Pyrenees mountains and, conversing in

French, the future German Slow Food leader was won over by Petrini's passion for food and optimism and went back to found a small convivium in his home town.

The development of other national associations also owed a lot to Italian connections. The co-leaders of the San Francisco Slow Food convivium, Lorenzo Scarpone and Carmen Tedesco, are both of Italian extraction, which has had cultural and practical implications for the development of Slow Food in that city. Many of the convivium activities have an Italian flavour while Scarpone, who comes from an Abruzzo farming background, has used his expertise in Italian wine to introduce lesser known Italian vintages to local members and supporters. He was attracted to Petrini because of the latter's empathy for the farming community. 'He talked about respecting the farmers. As farmers in Abruzzo we were second-class citizens.'

It is noticeable that the three largest national associations outside Italy – US, Germany and the UK – have long had a fascination with Italy, and this has been significant in the development of Slow Food in these countries. At one level it is apparent in practical and organisational ways. In addition to the San Francisco convivium there are other Italians involved in local convivia. In London, the 'Mediterraneo' convivium was set up in association with the Italian Cultural Institute. It is no surprise that one of the largest convivia in Germany is in Munich, jokingly referred to by some Germans as 'the biggest city in northern Italy'. At another cultural level, however, the significance of Italy is deeper and more pervasive. Otto Geisel told me that a 'love of Italy' was the initial attraction for German members, particularly in the south of the country, who wanted to take the opportunity offered by Slow Food to enjoy good pasta, olives and wine. The long history of German travellers to Italy, notably Goethe, is similar in some ways to the experiences of nineteenth-century British travellers, while in the US the love of Italy is equally apparent. In these countries, aspects of Italian food and lifestyle are evident in the convivia activities. Indeed the importance of this image of Italy for these national associations amounts to what might be called an 'imagined slow community'. In this adaptation of Benedict Anderson's view of the nation as an imagined external place, the values of 'slow living' attributed to Italy now take on a more immediate meaning and application in the different agendas adopted by Slow Food members in their respective countries.[2]

There are many positive aspects to this idea. An important part of Slow Food's founding philosophy, evident in its Manifesto and in much of its own internal language, is the 'civilising' function of food, derived from Italian traditions, in which time spent eating together not only provides conviviality but a respite from the industrialised 'fast life', and the basis for an alternative way of living. This idea, with real roots in Italian history, is crucial to Slow Food's alternative cultural politics, while it has been particularly attractive to the US, UK and Germany and other countries trying to rediscover the importance of food as part of their own cultures. By contrast, Slow Food has found it more difficult to recruit members in France, partly because it is seen as an Italian movement led by a 'charismatic guru', and partly because France enjoys more self-confidence over its food culture. According to Mike Tommasi of Slow Food France: 'In France people have the idea that there is no food crisis and that food here is the best in the world.' The strength of Slow Food France lies in the south, in places like Montepellier and Perpignan, perhaps because of their closer proximity to Italy.

But there are also drawbacks, as John Dickie has argued in *Delizia*. Some of the representations of Italian food and culture are nostalgic and simplistic and lead to distorted accounts of what authentic Italian food is, and even what Italians get up to at the dinner table. For example, you never see Italians dipping bread into bowls of olive oil nor do they include the range of ingredients that British or American 'Italian' trattorias serve up. Italian food is made of simple ingredients, some like the Tuscan dish *ribollita*, a bean and cabbage stew, or *polenta*, staple diet of the Italian poor, yet the authenticity of '*cucina povera*' is often overplayed, with the rural origins, as Dickie has argued, less significant than that of the great Italian cities in the wider history of Italian food.[3]

In any event, the need for national associations to develop their own food cultures and be less reliant on Italy is a necessity for the long-term future of Slow Food. From Terra Madre onwards, this started to become more apparent, and by the time of the Mexico Congress in 2007 it was a debate that had advanced further, with the rise of Slow Food USA and other associations bringing with them different food traditions, histories and political cultures.

In addition, the transformation that Slow Food had undergone since the first Terra Madre in 2004 brought a new, less Western, focus, with the prospect of developing an international network. Since 2004 new convivia have been set up in Kenya, Uzbekistan, Romania and Mexico. This meant that the nature of Slow Food's membership was changing significantly, with members now in 126 countries. The proportion of members in developing countries, set against the membership as a whole, had grown from 8 per cent in 2003 to 22 per cent in 2007, largely due to the impact of Terra Madre which had helped bring an overall increase of 362 per cent in members from these countries. Before Terra Madre, of course, Slow Food had very limited contact with producers and was justifiably seen as a Western organisation. This increased presence in the developing countries was significant for Slow Food's wider composition as well as its global impact.[4] After Terra Madre Slow Food became a political movement with a recognisable cause. According to Cinzia Scaffidi: 'There are lots of people who say "I'm a Slow Food supporter" who never take out a membership card. But they feel they are a supporter of Slow Food.' According to Scaffidi, after Terra Madre members and supporters started to express a stronger Slow Food identity, for example, making the assertion 'I am slow', in stating a preference for a different way of living.

Carlo Petrini's vision of Slow Food has also developed in the years since 2002. With 'good, clean and fair', Slow Food now had a clear defining set of principles that were able to bring greater ideological clarity to the ideas of eco-gastronomy, biodiversity and sustainability. The move towards a new 'network' was also very significant for the future organisation of Slow Food, and one of the defining features of its development as an organisation is its dual purpose as a political movement *and* a global network. However, its own internal structure left many unresolved dilemmas in place. Slow Food had set up an International Congress which was to meet infrequently in its early years, during which time its international composition had expanded significantly. Further, as its organisational hierarchy was based around the International President (Carlo Petrini), Vice-Presidents (Alice Waters, Giulio Colomba and Vandana Shiva), and the International President's committee (an international council made up of representatives from national associations, national councils and the local convivia), there was greater movement from below for more autonomy.

Existing methods of accountability allowed convivia to elect representatives to the national boards. National representatives, usually senior members such as the chair and secretary, would be represented at International Council meetings in Bra. This was weighted to allow the more numerous national associations better representation, which reflected their stronger membership. In addition, prior to 2007, a national office could only be established once the number of members had passed 1,000. This was significant for the degree of autonomy in each national association; those with memberships under 1,000 effectively received their directions from the international committee in Bra. With the number of Congress delegates decided by the strength of each national association,[5] the uneven dispersal of members meant that Italy and the US between them had half the delegates to the Mexico Congress in 2008, with Italy a third of all delegates.

The evolution of the Slow Food movement and the development of its network put more strain on the organisation, as it prepared for the Mexico Congress in 2007. The membership fee, for example, had been thought too high for developing countries so a new type of membership was made available to reflect the growth of the movement there. Now there was further consideration given to making the membership structure more flexible. With the typical age of Slow Food members between 45 and 60, greater emphasis was placed on recruiting younger members. More fundamentally, Petrini's aim of creating local food communities depended on strengthening the 'network', re-focusing the convivia around the producer rather than the consumer.

Slow Food's organisational structure, following its foundation as an international movement in Paris in 1989, had subsequently evolved through the second International Congress held in Venice in 1990, the third Congress which was held in Orvieto in 1997, and the fourth in Naples in 2004, which, with delegates from over 50 countries, marked a significant expansion of the movement. In Naples, the news was announced of the first Terra Madre, to be held the following year, and of the idea – which Petrini later called a little 'lie', as he did not expect to pull it off – of holding the next Congress outside Europe, in Mexico.

Ultimately the ability of the Slow Food international office to go ahead and hold the fifth International Congress in Puebla, Mexico, marked a decisive and ambitious turning-point in Slow Food's development as a movement, and reflected the intention of Petrini and the Slow Food leadership to shape the further transformation of the movement and address its organisational weaknesses.

In the pre-Congress document, circulated in advance to national associations, with its carefully chosen title, 'Taking Back the Earth, the Moon and Abundance', Petrini set out his new vision. 'After Terra Madre we found ourselves with a new, very different reality and a very complex one at that ... So both Slow Food and its mission must undergo further adaptation to this new reality or else risk missing out on important opportunities.'[6]

The 'adaptations' Petrini had in mind can be put into three categories. First, there was a need for ideological clarity in the movement's principles and objectives. Slow Food, Petrini reminded the delegates, was first and foremost an eco-gastronomic movement, one which felt compelled to intervene as the planet faced some of its biggest challenges, and where the understanding of food was rooted in the conditions and aspirations of those who worked the land. By 'the moon', Petrini was alluding to the importance of ideas, even of utopias, and stressing a holistic and critical worldview, where there is 'no fear of dreaming, of inventing, of finding connections between things that seem disparate from each other...'.

Slow Food, Petrini argued, was involved in a 'small cultural revolution' that was sufficiently adaptable and complex to take on a growing presence in different parts of the world. Eco gastronomy was made possible by the complex unity between pleasure and responsibility, for him a defining duality, even perhaps a dialectical relationship unique to Slow Food, encapsulated by the 'good, clean and fair' principles. Pleasure was not a hedonistic set of desires removed from an environmental and economic context, but was informed by education, whereby the 'sensory characteristics' were trained and reawakened to resist the threat to pleasure by the standardisation of food. Pleasure was also rooted in cultural tradition and we need to be aware, Petrini pointed out, that 'what is good for me is not necessarily good for someone from another part of the world, a product as he is of another culture'. The idea of pleasure, of what is 'good', 'must be as democratic as possible, accessible to everyone, and sought out daily'.

Pleasure, in this democratic and open definition, was also linked to responsibility because of the 'respect (for) the ecosystem and biodiversity through all the phases of its production and distribution chain, no less protecting the health of producers and consumers'. Pleasure matched with responsibility was therefore incompatible with industrial agriculture, 'monocultures', genetically modified organisms, and products that have travelled excessively and unnecessarily. Pleasure linked to responsibility, according to Petrini, should also be reflected in social justice and 'respect for workers and their know-how, of rurality, of decent living conditions and suitable compensation for work done, of accessible prices, of gratification in producing well and in consuming quality products, of the definitive liberation of farmers, of the right to seeds'.

The link between pleasure and responsibility helps explain the more political focus of Slow Food's position and reflects the influence of Terra Madre and the movement's attempt to shift its emphasis towards producers in the developing world. In general Petrini wanted more ideological clarity while not inhibiting the scope for idealism. Petrini's statement carries a strong sense of the ideological critique of a system, with a clear idea of an alternative, with no fear of using 'utopia' to imagine what an alternative society could be like, which has the effect of a pre-figurative politics. There is also an interrogation of the language and values which drive the global economic system. The understanding of 'abundance' was a case in point, according to Petrini:

> The system, or those that govern us, have made abundance something to watch with suspicion; wealth, excess (leading to waste), taking and taking without questioning what remains for the earth and for others or what will no longer renew itself. Abundance, in this sense, as designated by our society, creates

inequities, a developed world and developing world, an earth that will no longer be able to give as much as it has. Take back abundance means first and foremost understanding the meaning of this word which connotes generosity ... Abundance is that which we must give back to the Earth, and doing so in a way that can satisfy us with harvests that use rich, good, clean and fair. It is a concept that must be conceived in terms of sustainability.

The second area of reform outlined by Petrini was to develop the *local* dimension of Slow Food's work. This idea was to be deeply rooted in the idea of a food community as Slow Food's organisational form, but it was also derived from the need to 're-localise production and consumption'. His argument was that there is now the possibility of developing or strengthening local economies in ways which protect biodiversity. The local community is the place where traditions can be kept alive, where informed relationships between producers and consumers (or 'co-producers') can be developed and knowledge and experience can be circulated. Yet this re-localisation is also a political response to globalisation. Indeed Petrini was committed to a 'new idea of economy', one which 'built upon agriculture ... local communities, their food, their culture, their traditions and practices and the lands in which they live'. 'The market economy as we know it and as it has been determined by globalization', he continued, 'is revealing gross limits – both from the standpoint of the sustainability of its activities and from its way of producing wealth.'

The economic alternative to a centralised and industrialised agriculture was to be a 'local economy' or 'nature-based' economy, an idea which, according to Petrini, 'had not been invented from thin air', but had the backing of 'economists and experts'. The output of this 'local economy', 'an ecological, organic or humane economy', would no longer be producing waste 'but a more immaterial flow, the enjoyment of life'. Petrini used the examples of the different types of farmers' markets in the US, Italy (the Mercatale in Montevarchi) and France to show ways in which 'micro-economies' are already working. These micro-economies are 'compatible with their own eco-system, their own countrysides, their own biodiversity'. There is an economic model based on the local food community which reflects alternative values of 'fairness, generosity, openness to others and to diversity'.

For Petrini, much needed to be done for Slow Food to make this a more widespread reality, but it signalled the direction the movement needed to take from the Mexico Congress. The organisational form that would allow Slow Food to move further in this direction was the idea of a network, first raised at Terra Madre of 2006. This was the third major reform proposed by Petrini in his pre-Congress document. He argued that the network should have a loose structure, even to some degree be 'anarchic', in order to avoid ideological rigidity or organisational bureaucracy and to allow creativity on behalf of the activists. He accepts, however, that some structure is needed for members to share common goals, to communicate and exchange ideas and information, and to meet at international, national and local levels. Petrini also describes Slow Food in the Mexico document as a 'virtuous multi-national', one

> that is powerful and able to counter the negative tendencies [of globalisation] that, I am sure, will always include more people, institutions and associations who are willing to collaborate. This network will be the catalyst for realizing our goals. The network will allow us to spread – according to local culture – our message of peace, well-being, innovation, tradition and pleasure.

The crucial part of the network remains the convivium as the local base of Slow Food, the point at which activists come together with producers. It is the convivium which is the linchpin of the network, where activists raise awareness, organise local markets and start local projects, and, through involvement with Slow Food, bring issues to international attention. However, Petrini felt that many convivia were restricted to what he called 'classic gastronomy', that is, 'they limit themselves only to dinners and convivial meetings'. Although these were worthwhile in themselves, because they help generate knowledge and awareness amongst convivia members, they were unable to address wider issues within the local community. In a way this was a recognition that although Slow Food since Terra Madre had shifted its emphasis towards a political movement, this had not been fully reflected at a local level. Petrini's concern also resonated with the outlook of Marc Aerni and other convivium leaders who did not want to be merely hosting wine tastings and attracting people who just wanted to eat well.

Petrini wanted the convivia to be organising more events which contributed towards building a new kind of economy based on local food communities. He drew on the experiences of the education classes Slow Food had organised, notably taste workshops, and Master of Food courses, and saw education as the key to change. This would need to go beyond knowledge of products to engage in a more deep-rooted programme aimed at changing people's behaviour and lifestyles in respect of the food they eat. The perspective Petrini began to outline entailed a significant transformation in the outlook of the convivia, though for him, this was a natural development from the work Slow Food had been developing over recent years.

In the pre-Congress document, therefore, Petrini proposed replacing 'convivia' with 'food communities'. This was driven by his view that we should no longer think of Slow Food activists as 'consumers' but as 'co-producers'. 'The era of the consumer is over; he literally consumes the world and is the key figure in a market-economy-based society; he is the primary accomplice in the destruction being done to the earth.' On the other hand, the co-producer, 'educating himself, knowing products, the producers themselves, and methods for better feeding himself and polluting less ... becomes concretely and individually the engine of true change'.

As co-producers, the work of the convivium members would be transformed through dialogue, and more direct contact with the producers. The relationship is reciprocal since 'the co-producer is the companion the producer lacks in order to make a true local economy that is community based and good, clean and fair'. The preservation or excavation of knowledge is a crucial part in the fostering of the identity of local food communities. Petrini even talks about 'slow knowledge' where, through 'archiving' and 'cataloguing', video documentaries and other methods, the historical knowledge of farmers and other producers is preserved and utilised for the local economy. The dependence on local and historically based knowledge was sustained by the belief that 'popular wisdom ... teaches us good sense'.

This transformation in the role of the convivia demands a strong civic duty and sense of responsibility to their own communities. Petrini even goes as far as to suggest ethical banking systems that would contribute towards community development, and 'slow money' based on reciprocal services and exchange of skills. Oral communication, face-to-face meetings and contacts, would be pivotal in this.

Yet the food communities are also to be part of an international network, sustained by global exchanges, building on the example of the Terra Madre blog and through innovative use of the web. The University of Gastronomic Science should also be viewed as a resource for the movement, Petrini argued, a meeting point for international students and a knowledge base, with the students the future members of the international association.

The biggest challenge however was to turn the convivia into food communities. In particular Slow Food had to find a way of incorporating the large Terra Madre food communities into the movement. In some countries, notably Eastern Europe, Kenya and other countries in the developing world, the food communities in these cases had not previously been involved in Slow Food, but their delegates had returned home and started local convivia after Terra Madre. In other cases the convivia had not yet incorporated or formed a close enough relationship with the producers; this was the case in many Western countries, notably the UK and the US.

Petrini was doubtful that the convivium 'as we know it' can realise the new objectives of the movement. They had to go beyond organising dinners, 'to undertake activities that are a little more complex, to look for partners and starting points outside of the movement and outside their own realm of experience'. The only solution, then, according to Petrini, was to change the name of the convivium to 'community'. He accepted that it was a 'momentous change' and acknowledged that different views would be heard at the Congress. However, he believed that 'community' better describes 'what we can be and in many cases already are at the local level'. He talked of the mix of convivium leaders, volunteers, ordinary members, producers, restaurateurs, farmers, journalists, and environmentalists, who often come together at Slow Food gatherings but who may not be members. A 'community' rather than a 'convivium' can

> welcome everyone, operate on a shared sense of identity ... Community seems to me a term much richer in meaning than convivium and could allow us to get past perceptions of Slow Food as elitist in certain countries and of the dinner ritual that can become the only occasion to come together and the only real activity the convivium organises – it's somewhat less than what we are seeking.

At the UK meeting in London in June 2007, which discussed arrangements for the Mexico Congress, there were mixed views about the proposed change of name. The UK was one of the countries where Slow Food was still often regarded as elitist and also suffered from weaker relationships between members and producers. Some of the UK members wanted to retain the name convivium because it was 'unique'; in a political culture where pleasure was often regarded with suspicion, the term 'convivium' was also intriguing for those used to more mundane forms of organisation. Some were suspicious of the term 'community' because of 'religious' connotations. However others were more positive about the proposed new word, which would allow the local organisations to escape the image of a dinner club, while others found the term 'convivium' embarrassing. In the event no definitive conclusion was reached, instead a typically British compromise ensued whereby the change of focus was accepted, but a willingness to keep the name of convivium also persisted.

The transformation of the local groups was to be part of a wider attempt to open up Slow Food's membership structure. A more flexible membership structure which reflected the circumstances of those in poorer countries was proposed, as well as a lower student membership fee. In addition, a new way of communicating between the international organisation and the national and local associations was proposed by Petrini. This would mean the end of the quarterly editions of *Slow*, which was sent to all members and published in six different languages, at considerable cost, and its replacement with an annual almanac of Slow Food events. Other forms of communication at international level would be used to maintain contact. These changes allowed more space for national associations to organise initiatives, and, by reducing the number of members needed to set up a national association, would allow for more innovations at local and national level.

In the event, the Mexico Congress, attended by over 600 delegates from 49 countries, and taking place shortly after a flooding disaster in the Tabasco state, endorsed most of the main changes proposed by Petrini, while opening up important questions over the future of the movement. Petrini's announcement that this would be his last period of office as International President, while taking some delegates by surprise, signalled the maturity of the movement. Perhaps it had now reached the situation where it no longer depended upon the charisma and leadership of a main figure. The Congress confirmed the importance of the wider global context the movement had been seeking for some time. Petrini's opening speech sought solidarity with the people of the flooded area, and events surrounding the Congress looked to develop a strong identification with the local culture, with visits to the Cholula Pyramid, a concert in the Cathedral, cocktails and dinners consisting of local specialities becoming important parts of the unofficial agenda. Judging by the speeches of the delegates, the idea of eco-gastronomy and the more popular language of 'good, clean and fair', was cemented as the general philosophy of the movement, whether it was used in relation to the condition of Mexican farmers, fishing in Norway, or salmon in the Irish sea. Following Terra Madre, then, the Mexico Congress confirmed the internationalism of the movement and a stronger connection with food communities as Petrini had hoped.

The Congress itself was similar to the gatherings of other movements with its motions, speeches, and rule changes, though the conviviality of the event with long lunch breaks and superlative dinners surpassed most activist gatherings. At times the atmosphere appeared more like a rally with few points of disagreement, virtually no conflict, and many unanimous motions. Yet the Congress did open up some important questions which are likely to shape the direction of the organisation's future. First, the growth of the US association was more evident than before, partly in the role Erika Lesser, SFUSA's leader, played during the Congress. After introducing the whole event, she was also crucial in chairing sessions and introducing one of the most significant interventions at the Congress, involving the US students, which helped shift the conference agenda in the direction of young people. The youth delegation from the US announced proposals to establish an international student network. This was driven by the success of 'Slow Food on Campus', launched by student members of Slow Food, which had included the sustainable food project at Yale University.

The University of Gastronomic Sciences has around 300 students covering 30 different nationalities, 13 of which were represented in Mexico. In a group presentation to the delegates, they described the importance of the international- ism of their student environment for deepening understanding of global issues, leading to mutual exchanges and forms of solidarity. Their internationalism was partly driven by the experiences they had gained on international 'stages': field trips to locations as different as Africa, Sicily, Scotland and Japan. Together with the US students they presented a series of challenging objectives for the Slow Food movement, which included involving young people in the work of the local convivia; developing university-based convivia; investing in young farmers through a stronger relationship between the university and Terra Madre communities; integrating young people into the Slow Food leadership, with the objective of getting a young person on the board of every national association; and creating new methods of communication and engagement befitting an international youth movement. This involvement of young people was one of several ways in which the Italian hierarchy appeared to be weakening its grip on the movement, and Petrini's response, mindful perhaps of his own political apprenticeship and aware that most social movements are driven by youth, was to announce that the next Terra Madre in 2008 would include a parallel meeting of young people and farmers.

Petrini's pre-Congress proposal to change the name of the local group from 'convivium' to 'community' never saw the light of day. The week before, Carlo Bogliotti had told me that the intended change was a 'provocation' on Petrini's part, to shift the attention from critical consumers to food producers. In the event Petrini talked enthusiastically about the positive message given by the name 'convivium', which he attributed to the movement's distinctive emphasis on pleasure. The term 'convivium', he realised, meant more in countries with less robust food cultures, in the US, the UK and Germany in particular. The term 'food community' could give rise to problematic translations, with the German and English words having a different emphasis from the Italian. It was also unfair, some delegates asserted, to associate the term 'convivium' with elitist dinner parties; it had a more substantial set of associations.

The Congress also went some way towards developing the idea of the network. With Petrini standing down in 2011, delegates were asking not only who his successor would be but whether there would be one leader (and, indeed, whether he or she would be Italian), or whether there would be a decentralised structure, with the international and national offices helping to 'facilitate' the work of the associations and the convivia.

Slow Food had already conceived the idea of the network from Terra Madre. In Petrini's view, which was aided by the work of Bogliotti and others, Terra Madre had brought together a network of producers, consumers (or 'co-producers') and academics. The purpose of this 'network of gastronomes' was, in accordance with other theories of the network, to be more open and 'self-sustaining', to exchange knowledge and experiences through increasing both its *intensity* (that is, the ability of the 'nodes' or units, say the 'food community' or convivia, to reach more people) as well as its *extent*[7] – the ability to expand, to create and develop new nodes. In the case of the Terra Madre network, the global reach of Slow Food, and the different knowledges and experiences of the producers, were intended to create mutual understanding as well as strengthen its political impact so the network would be more likely to achieve its goals, to create what Petrini likes to call a 'community of destiny'. The interdependence of Slow Food's network would contrast with the global power of multi-nationals.

Applying this kind of network to the decision-making structures of the organisation as a whole was, however, more complex. With the hierarchy of the organisation remaining in Italy, the rapid expansion of the movement in the US and other countries, and a strong visionary leader whose tendency was to discuss new projects with close colleagues in Bra, the democratic structure of the organisation in regard to decision-making and accountability is uniquely difficult.

Though Slow Food has not suffered from the kind of splits that have plagued other movements, there have been cases where national associations have been reorganised or convivia suspended. Some of these were to do with business issues where the Slow Food logo had been used inappropriately (for example to support private business ventures), or used without permission, as had happened in Switzerland and Germany. In other cases, where the organisation had expanded at a quicker rate than the democratic structures, there was difficulty in holding leaderships to account and bringing forward new generations; this was apparent when convivia underwent the transition between the classical gastronomic position and the development of Slow Food as a global movement. In Autumn 2007 the German board of Slow Food was reshuffled following differences over how to expand and develop a more public political position.

In a movement based in over 100 countries, with different cultures and histories, there is the potential problem of respecting diversity while ensuring unity and democracy. Naomi Klein had encountered this problem in the emerging structure of the World Social Forum in Porto Alegre, where new forms of participatory democracy and international networks of local political groups were brought together.

Perhaps the real lesson of Porto Alegre is that democracy and accountability need to be worked out first on more manageable scales within local communities and coalitions and inside individual organisations. Without this foundation there's not much hope for a satisfying democratic process when ten thousand activists from wildly different backgrounds are thrown on a university campus together.[8]

Slow Food does not have the range of different organisations of the World Social Forum, but its diverse global network does contain different styles of leadership and political participation. These were evident during the Mexico Congress when US and British delegates objected to a motion proposed by Italian members on the basis that an English translation had not been discussed in advance. One of the objectors was Michael Dimock, the first chair of Slow Food USA, who also chaired Slow Food's international council, a job he sometimes found difficult as some Italian representatives would make long-winded speeches and would be offended if he attempted to cut them short.

Dimock told me that he welcomed the decision to modernise Slow Food's structure. He believes that Slow Food should no longer think in terms of core centres but about ways of facilitating information between regions. 'People don't get information early enough.' This would mean the New York office, for example, being a 'service centre' for the SFUSA network, thereby giving more autonomy to members on the ground across the US. 'We need to figure out how to empower regions', says Dimock. In the future he thinks there will be no single person succeeding Petrini as International President ('we will have failed if there is'), and proposes a 'rotating leadership' or a 'roundtable of leaders'. While he believes the international offices should always remain in Bra ('everybody loves Italy'), he thinks a more open democratic structure would also help promote diversity and allow different skills to be utilised.

This was also Petrini's idea. It appealed to his long-standing commitment to libertarian anarchism and the Italian tradition of 'associationism', the natural organisational form that would allow the 'healthy foolishness' he had always regarded as vital for the development of the organisation to flourish. 'We are strongly anarchic' he told the Congress delegates in Mexico. 'We don't have the ambition of being a political party.' Indeed, he endorsed more freedom and anarchy for the convivia and urged delegates to come forward with new initiatives. 'Ideas are good – use them. Let our ideas be expressed.'

Part Three
Places

7

Rediscovering the Local

S LOW FOOD HAS ATTEMPTED to articulate a politics rooted in local identity, traditions and cultures. Such a position, which suggests a distinctive 'politics of place', questions recent accounts of globalisation which see 'the local' as mainly an appendage to 'the global', driven and shaped by global economies, cultures and trajectories. Other interpretations, along a similar theme, have talked of a 'global village', whereby access to the benefits of globalisation is assumed to have produced increasingly common cultures and experiences. These interpretations underestimate the durability of local – and to some extent national – cultures and identities. Moreover, they preclude the possibility of the local itself articulating a distinctive identity which both assimilates and helps inform global forces rather than merely opposing or seeking protection from them. Such a position implies, as Doreen Massey has argued, a local politics based on place which goes beyond 'localism'. 'There is a need to rethink the "place" of the local and to explore how we can rearticulate a politics of place that both meets the challenges of a space of flows and addresses head-on the responsibilities of "powerful places" such as global cities.'[1] She argues that this more 'interdependent' idea of local places, which 'are not only the recipients of global forces, they are the origin and propagator of them',[2] would transform the political capability of locality. She envisages more awareness of the implications of local happenings, more collective responsibility for issues of public concern and more openness in the understanding of how local places can influence wider global issues.

Massey was talking primarily of cities, but her argument can be applied to other local places. In fact, as Massimo Montanari has written, food cultures as expressions of local identity are complex and there is no simple, fixed idea of 'rootedness':

> Every culture, every tradition, every identity is a dynamic, unstable product of history, one born of complex phenomena of exchange, interaction, and contamination. Food models and practices are meeting points amongst diverse cultures, the fruit of man's travels, of commercial markets, techniques, and tastes from one part of the world to another.[3]

The significance of this for Slow Food lies in the way in which food is a source of identity often in conflict with the powerful forces underpinning globalisation, which erode local traditions and impose corporate monocultures. The mass migration from rural areas to the city in recent years may be seen as a direct outcome of the development of the corporate economy and the destruction of traditional agriculture, the exploitation of land and the continual replacement of people by machinery. The links between rural and urban places are increasingly being shaped by the forces of globalisation.

Slow Food's emphasis on 'the local' is driven by its commitment to local knowledge, the importance of long-standing local memory for the maintenance of artisan skills and food production, the significance of local identity in defining a sense of place and the respect for biodiversity of land and produce, notably in the preservation of nature against its destruction by industrial agriculture. Increasingly within the Slow Food movement, there is a recognition of diversity in the ways in which food is produced and celebrated, while territory becomes a site of resistance and identity. During September and October 2007, students at the University of Gastronomic Sciences embarked on a month-long bike and boat tour of the River Po, in commemoration of Mario Soldati's TV documentary 'Viaggio nella Valle del Po', where 50 years earlier the writer and broadcaster had travelled in search of authentic foods. The students retraced Soldati's steps, crossing 13 provinces and 4 regions. They found deteriorating ecological damage along the river, and the effects of chemical agriculture, but also the persistence of some strong local food cultures.

An important aspect of Slow Food's commitment to 're-localisation' is the French concept of *terroir* which has been used to explain the way in which local areas have been characterised by distinctive natural conditions (including, for example, soil, climate and vegetation) and cultural factors (for example, particular traditions and knowledge) specific to the ways in which food is cultivated and cooked. According to Janet Lymburn:

> Culinary *terroir* is a concept that captures the spirit, romance and language of food and drink and recognises the role heritage and culture play in our culinary lives. At its simplest the glass of wine that we enjoy is a reflection of the environment that it was grown in ... If we think of *terroir* in a wider context than this, it also reflects the personality of the region the wine was grown in, the culture and heritage of a particular community and their constantly evolving agricultural practice.[4]

It is this idea of *terroir* which has been fundamental to the wine and gastronomic traditions of France. In August 1999 when José Bové led a group of sheep farmers in Millau, France, to drive their tractors through a partially constructed branch of McDonald's, they saw themselves defending their local culture and economy. According to Naomi Klein, they were asserting their 'right to local democracy and cultural diversity in a world governed increasingly by the principles that govern McDonald's; the same fare everywhere you go. It is about the right to distinct, uncommodified spaces – cultural activities, rituals, pieces of our ecology, ideas, life itself – that are not for sale.'[5]

Millau, in the South Aveyron region of France, is the home of Roquefort cheese, which, prior to Bové's intervention, had recently suffered from the imposition of US trade barriers in response to a refusal by the European Union to import hormone-fed beef. Roquefort was crucial to the local economy and the issue became a question of 'who decides the quality and integrity of the food we eat – local citizens or international trade institutions?'[6]

Carlo Petrini has acknowledged the importance of the idea of *terroir* in his own thinking. He has a long-standing interest in oral history and has spent many hours recording the experiences of folk musicians of the Langhe, as well as preserving ancient recipes. Arci Langhe organised trekking and other local initiatives aimed at discovering the land, and Petrini's strong identification with his local territory is also present in the early meetings of the 'Free and Meritorious Association of the Friends of Barolo' and became crucial in the development of Arcigola in the 1980s. After visiting the wine regions of Bordeaux, Burgundy, Alsace and Champagne, he and his friends learned the importance of territory in the heritage of French gastronomic culture at a time when Italy was undergoing a profound crisis in its own wine industry, in the aftermath of the methanol scandal. Petrini knew that the Langhe hills in his native Piedmont had a rich and ancient agricultural tradition but that it lacked the infrastructure of the French regions, which meant the quality of local produce had not been fully appreciated nor had tourism developed. Much of the work of Arcigola can be seen, therefore, as that of 'building' *terroir*.[7] Petrini and his comrades organised a series of 'agrarian assemblies' and wine conventions, with titles like 'Could the Langhe be to Piedmont what the Côte d'Or is to Burgundy?' 'What we wanted to do', Petrini explained, 'was promote the message that the Langhe was an emerging area with the quality to rival the best France has to offer.'[8]

On the back of these local initiatives, Arcigola, along with *Gambero Rosso*, the wine group, launched the first *Vini d'Italia*, the Italian wine guide, in 1987, which included 500 wine producers and around 1,500 wines. This has since become a prominent annual guide, but at the time it was a groundbreaking initiative aimed at rebuilding not only the status of Italy's wines, but also a sense of local identity and place amongst the wine communities. The activities around wine provided the breakthrough which continued with the development of the osteria movement, which had the objective of restoring and safeguarding 'the identity of the osteria as a place to take simple meals'. The opening of the *Osteria dell'Unione* in Treviso in 1981, the *Osteria del Boccondivino* in 1984, and the *Osteria del'Arco* in Alba in 1986, represented part of a renaissance of the osteria, while the *Osterie d'Italia*, since its first edition in 1990, has contributed to the sense of local identity inspired by food.

Some have accused Slow Food of presenting a nostalgic view of local places as a way of enhancing tourism and the marketing of local products. This underestimates the depth and complexity of its politics of place, while failing to address the more recent Slow Food presence in the countries of the South and its critical engagement with globalisation. As Parkins and Craig argue: 'Such connectedness – of place, people, history, culture – constitutes a dynamic set of social relations that is under threat by the changes represented by globalisation and its capacity to erase cultural specificities.'[9]

The problem of globalisation for this sense of local identity originated in colonialism and is now manifest in the power of multi-nationals to impose their own demands and brands at the expense of local skills and traditions. There are cultural as well as economic manifestations of this, with 'McDonaldisation' imposing its own dominant standardised norms, which erode local cultural differences. This has meant that the very term 'development' – as applied, for example, to 'developing countries', or even in the phrase 'sustainable development' – needs to be treated with caution. Slow Food, along with other critics of globalisation, hints at a different idea of local communities, one which looks for 're-localisation', free from the economic and cultural constraints of the global market.

From his home in Kentucky, the writer and poet Wendell Berry has written extensively about the importance of defending local identity against the law of the economic market and the technocratic certainties of the modern era. Berry's commitment to his own territory, in which he has contributed to the preservation of the local land and agriculture, is reflected in his emphasis on the diversity of local foods and ideas on how to revive the local economy. This is an argument for small-scale and decentralised local industries which would 'transform the products of our fields and woodlands and streams: small creameries, cheese factories, canneries, grain mills, furniture factories, and the like. By "small" I mean simply a size that would not be destructive of the appearance, the health, and the quiet of the countryside.'[10]

He argues that the small, decentralised units would make best use of the diversity of the land and asserts that this 'need for diversity' 'is the need of every American rural landscape that I am acquainted with. We need a greater range of species and varieties of plants and animals, of human skills and methods, so that the use may be fitted ever more sensitively and elegantly to the place.'[11] The existing policy (he was writing in 1988) was failing:

> The present practice of handing down from on high policies and technologies developed without consideration of the nature and the needs of the land and the people has not worked and it cannot work. Good agriculture and forestry cannot be 'invented' by self-styled smart people in the offices and laboratories of a centralised economy and then sold at the highest possible profit to the supposedly dumb country people. This is not the way good land use comes about.[12]

The arguments for smaller-scale industry in rural areas are nothing new or special to Slow Food. E.F. ('Fritz') Schumacher argued for similar solutions in 1973, in his renowned book *Small is Beautiful*. This was a work on economics and sustainability which took issue with the conventional view of judging economic success on the basis of higher GDP, often at the cost of ecological resources and built on cheap labour. Three decades ago, when such arguments were more heretical, Schumacher rejected the argument that the 'problem of production' had been solved – a 'fateful error' in his view. This had set humanity on a 'collision course' of ecological devastation and a degradation of individual skills and talents. Indeed, he saw the long-term costs of industrial agriculture some time before the arguments became mainstream.

> In our time, the main danger to the soil, and therewith not only to agriculture but to civilisation as a whole, stems from the townsman's determination to supply to agriculture the principles of industry. ... The question arises of whether agriculture is, in fact, an industry, or whether it might be something *essentially* different.[13]

His major contribution was to challenge what he called the 'idolatry of giantism', and to promote in its place 'the virtue of smallness'; though he did not advocate 'smallness' uncritically, the key question was 'what scale is appropriate?'[14] The problem was that 'the economics of giantism', effectively nineteenth century industrialism, were not able to solve the contemporary problems of the individual producer, which could now be understood by the phrase 'production by the masses, rather than mass production'.[15]

> We must learn to think of an articulated structure that can cope with a multiplicity of small-scale units. If economic theory cannot grasp this it is useless. If it cannot get beyond vast abstractions, the national income, the rate of growth, capital/output ratio, input-output analysis, labour mobility, capital accumulation: if it cannot get beyond all this and make contact with the human realities of

poverty, frustration, alienation, despair, stress, congestion, ugliness and spiritual death, then let us scrap economics and start afresh.

In response he proposed 'a new lifestyle, with new methods of production and new patterns of consumption; a life-style designed for permanence'.[16] This included 'biologically sound' production methods, and the development of small-scale technology and local ownership of industry. His ideas inspired subsequent environmentalists and the founding of Schumacher College in Devon, south-west England, which has hosted Slow Food leaders in its conference and seminar programmes.

Schumacher, like Berry, was a revered thinker for many delegates at Slow Food's Mexico Congress, which called for the 're-localisation' of food communities. The local assumed a more fundamental part of Slow Food's politics as the experiences of different communities became apparent. In his pre-Congress document, Petrini had outlined this objective of strengthening local food communities. In his powerful opening speech to the Congress (regarded by people close to him as one of his best), he once again returned to this theme. The alternative to the inequality created by global corporations would be the building and strengthening of local economies. This would not be easy and would require a clear political choice.

'Our association', he declared, 'will be in harmony with all those working at local level – traditions, legends, local memory will be preserved.' There could be no local economy, he said, without 'local culture' and 'local memory'. Traditional 'scientific' knowledge, whereby farmers – and here he repeated his view that they should be regarded as 'intellectuals of the earth' – would meet on equal terms with university professors. Investing in local farmers would be the best way of preserving biodiversity. He envisaged local areas having access to central services without needing to lose their most creative producers. He lamented the way Mexican farmers had been compelled to leave their country in search of work in California and the consequences this held for their local area. 'These people are taking their scientific knowledge to another country and Mexico loses its intellectuals.' Young people in particular needed to be won back to agriculture. He used Mexico as an example of how a local economy was already functioning and needed to be developed. Using the example of Puebla, where the public face of the historic centre showed McDonald's, the Italian Coffee House and Burger King, he suggested that a closer look would reveal a local subsistence economy at work, with local women making tortillas on the roadside. 'This economy is very strong. It is largely a female economy. It is not in the GDP, but it is a local economy which contributes a lot to the identity of the country. In Puebla women work autonomously in the streets; this means the local economy is strong.'

The emphasis on building the local economy was driven by the concept of food communities. Petrini announced the first farmer convivium in Mexico made up solely of workers. This was the community of cacao producers from Villahermosa, Tabasco, an area heavily affected by the floods. This producers' convivium would have the responsibility of organising and co-ordinating Slow Food activities in Mexico. It was one of the clearest indications of what Petrini meant by a 'food community' embedded in the local area and economy.

The importance of the local in the politics of Slow Food is evident in the varied expressions of identity around food, but it has taken on different meanings in the increasingly diverse countries and traditions where Slow Food now has a presence. In Western countries, for example, the local element is often expressed through a recovery of local, seasonal products, through the development of the farmers' markets, greater awareness of local produce and empathy for the producer in the face of global fast foods and supermarkets. The 'critical consumer', as we have seen, is the driving force of most of these initiatives. Convivium leaders have made significant efforts to raise awareness of local food traditions and convivia hold events aimed at restoring local memory and cultural traditions where, in the promotion of local tourism, they express a sense of place to outside visitors. In many ways this assumes a global significance through challenging the homogenising culture of mass tourism. The development of the *cittaslow* network has helped to provide a strategy for some of these initiatives. This network was started in Italy in 1999 when four Italian towns, Bra, Orvieto, Positano and Greve-in-Chianti, drew up a list of defining criteria (over 30 in all) that each aspirant slow town would need to meet. First there had to be less than 50,000 residents. Then they needed to meet quite strict criteria on environmental practices (including policies on pollution and waste), preserving open spaces, maintaining architecture or historic buildings, commitment to the cultivation and development of local produce, local hospitality, and on raising the awareness amongst the citizens of what it means to live in a slow town. The number of towns in the *cittaslow* network has grown to 55 in Italy, with 6 in the UK, 8 towns close to accreditation in Spain, 7 in Germany, 4 in Portugal and Poland, 3 in Belgium and 2 each in Norway, Australia and New Zealand. In Italy *cittaslow* has developed through a network of mainly centre-left administrations and, given the architectural, civic and gastronomic traditions, have stronger identities as slow towns. In Greve, deep in the hills of Chianti, with an *enoteca* (wine shop) on every street, free of fast food stores and with local produce prominent, there is an evocative image of Italian slow life.

The reasonably strict criteria allow for local particularities, which emphasise some of the local features above others. In the Norwegian town of Sokndal, a fishing community of 3,300 people near the North Sea coast where the specialities are salmon and trout, it is the local geology (including fjords) and the protected wooden houses that mark out the town's distinctive heritage. The promotion of local tourism is carefully cultivated and the English-language literature states that Sokndal 'does not have any visitors, but a lot of guests who visits (sic)'. The smallest slow town, Marihn, in the Mecklenburg area of Germany, with 260 residents, is marked by its distinctive buildings and gardens. In Australia, for the historic town of Goolwa, situated near the Lower Murray River in the Western Fleurieu peninsula, it is the culture and tradition of the Ngarrindjeri aboriginal community that provide a distinctive sense of place.

The British *cittaslow* network is run from the small English town of Ludlow, in Shropshire, which has a well-established food festival, a rich programme of local festivals and a thriving Slow Food convivium. The national UK Slow Food office was established there in December 2006. Its identity as a slow town is expressed through local food markets, festivals and hospitality. Like Sokndal it doesn't refer to tourists but to 'temporary residents'. According to Sue Chantler of Ludlow Slow Food convivium, *cittaslow* status

> has given Ludlow a focus for the very necessary sense of urgency in preserving and developing a way of life which is endangered, and which fits the slow philosophy so closely. It draws on local people who are probably already involved in other groups within the town, the residents association, the church, the 'Local to Ludlow' group, and unites their common interests into a cohesive framework.

The notice on the Ludlow website illustrates the idea behind this approach: '*cittaslow* is a way of thinking. It is about caring for your town and the people who live and work in it or visit it. It is about protecting the environment, about promoting local goods and produce, and about avoiding the "sameness" that affects too many towns in the modern world.' Chantler fears that Ludlow still faces 'great risks' from corporate chains seeking to buy up the empty shops in the town. Costa Coffee has already arrived and a Tesco Superstore is the first building to confront the traveller who embarks at Ludlow station. She believes that the arrival of more multi-nationals will jeopardise

Ludlow's 'vibrancy' and 'identity', derived from the local producers in the town.

Aylsham is a small Norfolk market town in the east of England, of 6,700 people, situated ten miles from Norwich. In 2004 it was granted *cittaslow* status as the second UK town after Ludlow. Aylsham is an unremarkable British town: it is not a North Norfolk tourist destination in the manner of neighbouring towns such as Burnham Market (dismissed by locals as 'Chelsea on Sea'). However, it is distinguished by some notable architecture and historic buildings. The desire to preserve this heritage, combined with its strong community traditions (there are more than 150 active associations in the town), was the driving force of its campaign to be a slow town. The process, in which towns have to demonstrate their commitment to the necessary criteria, was not easy. Aylsham did not share Ludlow's reputation as a centre of food excellence, which was closer to the Italian model. Furthermore, the *cittaslow* profile does not fit easily into British local government strategies of regeneration.

According to Susan Flack, of the Aylsham partnership and one of the leading campaigners behind the *cittaslow* initiative, the key purpose of the slow town is sustainability and preservation, rather than regeneration. 'It is not about changing things, but preserving things.' She says local residents are 'very protective about the town'. 'If you live in a really good place, you need self affirmation; we need to say "we were right to stay here".' What is needed above all, according to Flack, is a 'philosophy and spirit', things that do not come easily to the British mindset.

Flack, who also helps organise the local Slow Food convivium, first became interested in the movement when she saw Carlo Petrini on BBC TV and became 'seized by the idea'. Now that Aylsham has won *cittaslow* status, the philosophy of slow living is gradually permeating the life of the town. Local businesses such as Crawford's butchers and markets

have responded eagerly and their produce has been promoted
in various local initiatives. These included the 'Aylsham Big
Breakfast', held in early 2005, when 120 people crowded into
the town hall, over two sittings, and ate a full English breakfast
consisting entirely of local produce. The local baker and
butcher shops provided the food, and the jams were provided
by the Women's Institute. Mo Reynolds, the town clerk and
Slow Food enthusiast, fried 120 eggs. According to Flack, the
event epitomised a new spirit of friendship in the town; for the
first time, she said, people talked to strangers from different
walks of life. There was a 'buzz of conversation' and it was
a public display of Aylsham folk enjoying themselves. It was,
she said, 'an immensely jolly do'.

The Aylsham carnival, which had been revived in 2005
after a five-year gap, included a 'slow procession' through
the town. There were no fast food outlets on display; instead
stalls sold local produce. On another occasion, local school
children from Aylsham High School were involved in cooking
a meal from local produce for a conference; they made a big
enough impression to be invited to take part in a food festival
in Orvieto, one of the centres of Italy's *cittaslow* network.

Susan Flack is proud of Aylsham's *cittaslow* image (the
town received enormous press coverage at the time of the
announcement), while remaining pragmatic about the impact.
The town has not been transformed overnight, but its own
local identity has been strengthened, and Flack describes as
an example the local opposition to attempts to open a big
supermarket complex nearby. Controlling traffic has been more
difficult, as Aylsham is used as a passage to other towns, but
here too she is practical, arguing that if you cannot prevent
traffic coming to the town, then you can at least change the
way it behaves, so that it adapts to the town's ethos. For Flack,
it was Slow Food's simple philosophy which was crucial. 'It
has changed the way I live. When I go out now, I always ask:
why rush, to what purpose?'

The *cittaslow* network has played an important part in challenging the assumptions of 'fast life' at a local level and has engendered a sense of place as a response to global change. 'Re-localisation', through the revival of vibrant local traditions, has celebrated and articulated a sense of place, through alternative tourism, and recognition of the diversity of local land and architecture. The *cittaslow* network has developed its own momentum and has remained relatively autonomous from the Slow Food movement. It has depended to a large degree on local politicians and sympathetic mayors, and, as yet, only has a presence in a limited number of countries, while the problems facing bigger cities are outside its domain. It is the one dimension of the slow movement which is engaged in day-to-day practical politics. However, it has helped maintain an alternative philosophy in various ways. It presents, for example, an alternative to the impact of global tourism by articulating a view of place which is rooted in specific cultural and local traditions and forms of hospitality which help to foster greater understanding of local history and food.

In developing countries, on the other hand, where Slow Food has a presence, 'the 'local' has taken on a more practical and engaged commitment with producers and investment in local territory, out of economic necessity. In these cases, the 're-localisation' of place as a source of identity has a more fundamental meaning, related to the revival of food cultures with far-reaching implications for the parlous state of the local economies. In Transylvania, an agricultural economy which has historically suffered from the effects of communism and the more recent and rapid shift to market solutions, the revival of local food traditions has provided another way of reviving local places. The quality of the natural environment in a remote part of northern Romania – rich in natural resources and different varieties of wildlife and vegetation – that Akeroyd has called 'the lost landscape of Europe',[17] has been the catalyst for the revival of the local economy.

In the medieval Saxon villages in this area, Slow Food's work with local jam producers was crucial in getting new projects off the ground. The significance for its sense of place is, however, even more profound. This area of fertile soil, where bears, wolves and rich plant-life can still be found, and which has not undergone the industrialisation of other parts, was threatened with a plan by the Ceauşescu government in 1988 which would have meant the demolition of all the villages. In the event, this idea was only stopped by the Romanian revolution of 1989. Subsequently however, following the massive exodus from the villages to Germany (after the German government invited repatriation in 1990), the villages were in crisis, with many abandoned houses, and faced the possibility of losing their history and culture. The cheap land on offer for property speculators presented a new threat and by 1996 there were plans for a Dracula Theme Park in the area, which had the support of some prominent politicians and businessmen, who sought funding from Coca-Cola and beer producers, and which further threatened the natural landscape as well as the local identity. Raul Cazan, who did an MA thesis on the Dracula Theme Park idea and who later set up the Bucharest Slow Food convivium, attributed this development to the 'savage accumulation of capital', whereby selling land to multi-nationals is presented as the only form of development. He says that 'the whole academic environment opposed it' and that the 'Sustainable Sighosiara' campaign to prevent it happening was successful and driven by the belief that the local area of natural beauty could be developed in more sustainable ways. Prince Charles, whose trust had bought a cottage in Viscri, one of the Saxon villages, was amongst those who opposed it. Cazan, who was brought up in a 'Transylvanian paradise' of good, healthy food, says that the appeal of the multi-nationals was short-lived, because people were beginning to rediscover the value of their land.

Despite the damage done by communist projects, which had largely turned Romania into a huge brownfield site with state farms and large factories, and had imposed extreme food rations (six eggs per month, half loaf of bread per person, meat heavily restricted), there was an informal economy in the Saxon villages, where friends and family members would exchange goods and hide them to escape police controls. It was the preservation of this local cultural identity, which had strong historical roots, going back centuries, that was to be the focus of Slow Food's intervention as it attempted with the support of local trusts like Adept to rebuild the territory. In the village of Saaschiz, a variety of attempts are being made to preserve Saxon culture. A local museum which has traditional Saxon furniture has just opened behind a bar and restaurant. At a Saxon house abandoned in the exodus to Germany, Adept are refurbishing the building according to traditional design, which they will use for offices. An oral history project is also underway in a country where people are not used to talking about themselves publicly. With houses going for 15,000–20,000 euros it is not easy to cement the idea of traditional culture or sustain a strong community. During my visit, the problem was illustrated by the shooting of 'The Dark is Rising' in the village, a nostalgic children's film, which used artificial grass and brickwork. Slow Food, together with the many trusts and local groups working to preserve this and other villages, argue that the local identity here needs sustainable tourism.

Teodore Vaidasigan, who has spent most of his life in the village working in agriculture, told me about the strength of values in the close-knit Saxon village communities. A strong work ethic led to a very productive life working in the fields and whole villages were involved in local festivals. The religion and language of the Saxons were largely left alone by the

Romanian authorities in the post-war years and they had their own schools and neighbourhood groups. The healthy food was attributable to the land and the farming traditions and was one reason why, despite the early popularity of fast food, local food traditions have been maintained.

Food subsequently became part of alternative tourism and cannot be separated from the wider projects to create sustainable tourism. The exodus in the early 1990s was a blow to the strength of the community, but while newcomers moved into the villages, Vaidasigan believes there is scope for generating new tourism. In fact, prior to the early 1990s there had been little tourism, and, in any case, according to Gerda Gherghiceau, a Viscri resident, 'we didn't have the right to speak to tourists'. There were no hotels in Sighisoara, for example, the main town in the region prior to 1998, virtually no cars and few visitors. As tourism took off, demand for food increased. At first it was the demand for industrialised food, followed by a wider realisation that quality food, made in the traditional way, was near at hand.

Raul Cazan remembers going to McDonald's because he was impressed by the colours. 'They bought me with the lights and colours. During communism there was no light and no colour. Everything was grey and dark.' Cristi Gherghiceau also remembers the 'hours of queuing' at McDonald's: 'There was a frenzy for it.' Cristi, who is from Viscri, is now Slow Food's main organiser in Romania, providing the link between Slow Food events like Terra Madre, Cheese and local convivia activities, and the work of the Adept foundation which is supporting local businesses in the community. He discovered Slow Food while working for Adept, helping to protect biodiversity and rural development. After his family opened a bed and breakfast they started to think 'Let's try to promote food: who can advise us?' Subsequently, more traditional cottages in Viscri and other villages offered bed and breakfast accommodation, including traditional meals and an insight into the life of the village, where there is still an absence of cars and where the bells are rung daily and communal tasks carry on.

The campaign against the Dracula Theme Park can be seen as a major victory for a sense of local place over mass tourism, in a poor area which had never known prosperity and which was open to the exploitation of the market. Similar issues have faced Slow Food as it has established a local presence in other parts of Eastern Europe. In Poland, where agriculture had not been given over to the state on the scale of Romania, food was still strictly rationed and quality food had to be smuggled in car boots. The arrival of fast food brought a similar initial response. This time, in Jacek Szklarek's memory, it was the clean toilets that were an attraction of McDonald's, while 'it was something new to try'. Whereas in Romania there was no real restaurant culture under Ceauşescu, in Poland home cooking was more established and there was better access to quality resources. Some of the local eating places, such as the 'Milk Bars' which provided cheap food for workers under the regime, had continued after 1989 and were popular with students. 'At first there was a fascination with foreign restaurants, notably Italian, Spanish and Greek restaurants. Everyone wanted something new, something special', Szklarek says. More recently this interest has waned and there has been a greater appreciation of Polish bread and sausages, which has brought the possibility of local tourism. In Krakow, local restaurants have begun to prosper. Adam Chrzastowski, the chef at the Ancora restaurant, who has coached the national Polish culinary youth team in international competitions, predicts a gastronomic revival of local cuisine. He uses ancient recipes (such as one for crayfish soup) and serves traditional dishes, including venison, in a modern way. He sees the revival of local food as a consequence of better education about local food, and expects a bright future for Polish cuisine.

Slow Food's focus on local economy and local culture will appear to many as utopian; a view substantiated, perhaps, by Petrini's discussion of 'slow money' and 'ethical banking systems'. For conventional policy makers, including many from the left, who accept the implicit assumptions of neo-liberalism (summed up by the phrase 'we are all neo-liberals now'), Slow Food's local politics and local economy driven by food communities is a non-starter, unable to address either the big questions of famine and poverty or the necessity of stimulating free markets. But there are many contradictions with this position. Critics of the Italian economy, for example, often attribute the low numbers of McDonald's and Starbucks to a lack of enterprise on the part of Italian business, yet they recognise the value for tourism of traditional 'slow' Italian culture.[18]

One of Petrini's and Slow Food's habits of course is to talk positively of utopias, 'of thinking big and thinking positive ... no fear of dreaming, of inventing, of finding connections between things that seem disparate from each other'.[19] 'If there's one thing that Carlo Petrini has taught me it is that you have to believe in utopias', Carlo Bogliotti told me. However, most people who have known Petrini a long time told me that he was also a pragmatist. The idea of re-localisation needs imagination but it also demands a practical mindset, capable of getting things done and engaging with, rather than retreating from, global structures and processes. It requires belief in a different, positive and virtuous idea of globalisation.

8

Virtuous Globalisation

I N THE MID 1970s, in the same historical moment in which Carlo Petrini was becoming involved in the politics of social movements, Western societies found themselves undergoing major economic and social transformation. This was the beginning of what would later be called modern 'globalisation', with nation-states no longer able to organise their economies on the basis of the welfare system. Although global trade was not a new phenomenon, the rise of the global market meant a profound change not only in the economies of the West but in their social, cultural and political composition. Globalisation was to bring new forms of living and would change the political and cultural landscape. During the 1980s, the rise of Thatcherism in the United Kingdom, 'Reaganomics' in the United States and the 'Milano da bere' in Italy, contributed in their different ways to the seemingly irreversible trajectory of the free market.

The high tide of modern globalisation was the early 1990s, following the end of communism and the fall of the Berlin Wall. The countries of Eastern Europe sought new injections of capital to revive their economies and it seemed as if Francis Fukuyama's argument in *The End of History and the Last Man*, that there was a growing convergence of free market Western economies with liberal representative democracies, would be borne out. Indeed, even parties of the centre-left, such as Tony Blair's New Labour, accepted the rationale of neo-liberal hegemony. Whatever credibility the idea of the third way now holds for politics, it was used at the time to facilitate the shift of the European parties of the centre-left towards the market.

Subsequently however, from the mid 1990s, this early optimism began to fade. It was evident that globalisation was succeeding in some countries more than others, while there were very different types of capitalisms existing in different cultural and historical contexts. The economic crises in East Asia and Latin America in the late 1990s were evidence that globalisation, in its neo-liberal form, facilitated by the restrictions of the International Monetary Fund and the impositions of the World Bank, was failing many parts of the world. The contributions of Joseph Stiglitz, the former Chief Economist at the World Bank who warned of the costs and limits of global capitalism in *Globalisation and its Discontents*,[1] and of the political philosopher John Gray, who argued in *False Dawn* and other books that global capitalism was headed for chaos and destruction, reflected a growing concern about 'market fundamentalism'.[2] For many, the debts incurred by so-called developing countries were not being helped by IMF and World Bank policies on trade. According to Stiglitz, the IMF maintained an ideological position which insisted on the liberalisation of trade without tariffs on imports in developing countries, leading to the destruction of jobs and the local economies. This, he argued, was tantamount to 'kicking away the ladder'.[3]

In addition, the Millennium Ecosystem Assessment Report, published in 2005, warned of impending ecological disaster and of serious threats to biodiversity. The widespread imposition of so-called 'industrial agriculture' and the almost doubling of water consumption had created a real threat to the earth's resources. Globalisation had brought increasing inequality, particularly in Africa, and was preventing the development of local economies and agriculture. Other critics pointed to the connection between the global market and growing environmental crisis. Some returned to Marx, not for his prophecy of class struggle or his long-term solution of communism, but for his acute and evocative understanding of how the relentless expansion of global capitalism would sweep away all before it and constantly find new markets:

> The bourgeoisie cannot exist without constantly revolutionizing the instruments of production, and thereby the relations of production, and with them the whole relations of society. Conservation of the old modes of production in unaltered form, was, on the contrary, the first condition of existence for all earlier industrial classes. Constant revolutionizing of production, uninterrupted disturbance of all social conditions, everlasting uncertainty and agitation distinguish the bourgeois epoch from all earlier ones. All fixed, fast-frozen relations, with their train of ancient and venerable prejudices and opinions, are swept away, all new-formed ones become antiquated before they can ossify. All that is solid melts into air, all that is holy is profaned, and man is at last compelled to face with sober senses, his real conditions of life, and his relations with his kind.

'The need for a constantly expanding market for its products', Marx continued, in a passage which has a striking resonance for today's world, 'chases the bourgeoisie all over the whole surface of the globe. It must nestle everywhere, settle everywhere, establish connexions everywhere.'[4] From the late 1990s, a new generation of political activists took to the streets to protest against 'globalisation'. Naomi Klein's *No Logo* was the book of the moment, which helpfully clarified the problem and gave hope to the young protesters. In Seattle in 1999 the meeting of the World Trade Organisation was called off when over 100,000 people demonstrated. In Genoa in 2001, when the centre of the city was cordoned off to protect the G8 leaders at their summit, a young demonstrator, Carlo Giuliani, was killed, and police violence was widely condemned. In the aftermath of this protest local social forums were established all over Italy and became part of European and World Social Forum networks.

Slow Food shares this critical attitude towards globalisation and participated at different times in the European and World Social Forums. They share a similar critique of the neo-liberal global economy, and, in particular, opposed the pernicious argument that 'liberalisation' and 'free trade' were the only way forward for developing countries. Slow Food has also shared a common perspective with several NGOs, putting the blame for global inequality at the door of the World Trade Organisation, the World Bank and the International Monetary Fund for making poorer countries open up their markets to big foreign multi nationals rather than supporting poor farmers.

Slow Food argues that there is an alternative to the now dominant interpretation. According to Petrini, Slow Food grew as a 'critical reaction to the symptoms of incipient globalization'.[5] While the new movements often sought a 'no global' political identity and were often referred to as 'anti-globalisation movements', the reality was more complex, as they used a global network to mobilise support and the slogan of the 'anti-globalisation' movements, 'Another World is Possible', reflects the position which began to call itself 'New Global'.

Slow Food has pursued a different path to the oppositionism of some of the new movements, going beyond protest and attempting to root an alternative idea of 'the global' in the experiences of producers in the developing countries. Initially, Slow Food's differences with the other movements were mainly strategic. For example, the empathy many of Slow Food members feel for José Bové in his attempts to defend French agriculture against McDonald's and other corporations did not extend to some of the strategies adopted. Bové had often 'cast a spell over us', Petrini said, 'but when he adopts a strategy of direct action, he chooses the path of the guerrilla fighter, that we prefer not to take. That is not the slow style.

Our choice is to focus our energies on saving things that are headed for extinction, instead of hounding the new ones we dislike.'[6] Petrini also felt that the anti-global capitalist protests were essentially urban movements which had lost touch with the young farmers and agricultural workers whom Slow Food increasingly believes will be the drivers of social change. Otto Geisel, President of Slow Food Germany, offered a similar view on Slow Food's strategy when asked about the campaign against McDonald's in the Berlin suburb of Kreuzeberg. 'We try to make clear that we are not against anybody. For me, Slow Food is a movement with a basic idea, a network of producers and consumers. We want to promote this idea. I'm really convinced that this positive message has a better appeal and more power than always talking about bad meat.' Though Slow Food were involved in the campaign, it was important to keep the wider ideal alive.

As we know from previous chapters, it was standardisation, the threat to biodiversity, the industrialisation of agriculture and the degradation of the small producer that formed the basis of Slow Food's critique of globalisation. Terra Madre shifted attention to the conditions and lives of the producers in the poorer countries. The sharing of experiences between producers, chefs, activists and convivium leaders led to mutual understanding, and the joint commitment to action to support small farmers in practical ways. In doing so, it provided an alternative idea of globalisation. Petrini has since called this firstly 'positive' and then 'virtuous' globalisation. Effectively Slow Food was a global organisation acting on behalf of local food communities. According to Roberta Sassatelli, Slow Food is an 'international actor for the global promotion of the local'.[7]

There are similarities here too between Slow Food's idea of virtuous globalisation and Stiglitz's belief that globalisation can be made to work through finding a new 'balance'; what he calls a 'new *global social contract* between developed and less developed countries' (his emphasis).[8] Slow Food's strategy also differs from other initiatives aimed at ending global inequalities, such as Oxfam's *Make Poverty History* campaign which still focused primarily on aid (though it also called for changes in trade rules).

There are more similarities with the fair trade movement, through the need to educate Western consumers about the condition of the world's poor, as well as promoting alternative kind of trade:

> Fair Trade is trade with a difference. It's a way for us to help the world's poor every time we shop. With fair trade, producers in poor countries receive a decent return – a fair and stable price or wage for their products. Buying fair trade products is a way of taking practical action to bring about a better, more generous world.[9]

The idea of virtuous globalisation goes further, however, in its belief that a global system must work to aid the farmers, through a network of local economies which are on the one hand self-sufficient, but on the other sustained through forms of interdependent support. Terra Madre had provided the experience and inspiration for this approach. In many ways Slow Food's idea of virtuous globalisation was shaped by the experiences of Terra Madre, notably its internationalism, sharing of commitment, and empathy for the producer. As we saw earlier, in his opening speech to the Puebla Congress in 2007, Petrini expressed his solidarity with the Tabasco farmers who had suffered from the worst flooding in living memory in the previous two weeks. The first formal act of the Congress, Petrini declared, would be to express solidarity with the people of Tabasco with deeds not just words. Part of Tabasco, he said, 'belongs to Terra Madre'. All Terra Madre food communities would provide concrete help. It would be a 'tangible way for this community to take responsibility for revitalising the economy'. Elsewhere in his speech, Petrini talks of Slow Food being 'governed by Terra Madre'.

Terra Madre is not the only way in which Slow Food has articulated its alternative idea of globalisation. It participates increasingly in other global collaborative actions, on fair trade, and on support for the development of local economies which embody this alternative perspective. One main vehicle of Slow Food's virtuous globalisation is the Slow Food Foundation for Biodiversity set up in 2003. This is a development of the Ark and Presidia which had gone a long way in identifying the diversity of taste and flavours and then seeking to protect endangered foods and the communities which produced them. In many ways the setting up of the Slow Food Foundation reflects, at a different level, the shifts encountered by Terra Madre.

This Foundation, which is supported by the Tuscany Regional Authority and has its main office in Florence, was set up to protect resources and support projects around the world, increasingly in the less developed countries because the issues in these countries are not solely to do with preserving the 'quality of life, but actually saving lives, communities and cultures'. The support it offers includes small financial investments as well as helping promote and publicise projects and initiatives. However, the project provides the clearest evidence of Slow Food's alternative idea of globalisation based on practical and concrete projects aimed at preserving biodiversity, and building a network of support for food communities to help revive artisan work. This gives Slow Food a groundbreaking role, distinct from, though often in collaboration with, other organisations and NGOs. The evolution of the Slow Food Foundation for Biodiversity explains a lot about Slow Food's own development as an organisation, reaching beyond its Italian roots and looking to address bigger and more complicated questions, while seeking a more professional and scientific basis to its work.

The purpose of the Foundation is to help producers 'escape their increasing marginalisation in today's global market'.[10] It is to raise the profile of artisan producers and help them develop their production techniques and market their products so that they can become economically viable. The global significance of this work is to preserve the biodiversity contained in the variety of land products and cultures in the face of the monocultural dominance of neo-liberal globalisation. However, as Serena Milano, who has overseen the development of the Foundation, told me from her office in Bra, the project started out with more modest objectives. At the time the Ark of Taste was set up in 1996, the forerunner to the Presidia and the Foundation, 'we probably didn't know what the word "biodiversity" meant'. The term itself had only been used for about ten years and was associated with the impact of the large-scale industrialisation of agriculture that had rapidly taken place in the 1980s. Slow Food's lack of knowledge of biodiversity reflected its status at the time as primarily a gastronomic association.

The existing Ark of Taste started as 'just an idea'– 'an idea to preserve the taste of local products'. According to Milano, there was initially no plan to go further than this. 'There was no office, budgets, nothing. No criteria, just a symbolic idea.' Milano, however, took to the project and started to work on it in her spare time (she was then working in the print office, having joined Slow Food in 1996). 'I realised that we needed to involve more people, have better organisation and involve scientific experts.' She made contact with universities, but they were initially suspicious and she didn't get anywhere. Then at the Salone del Gusto of 1998, which was opened to the public for the first time, Slow Food organisers were struck by the press interest in the six or seven Ark products on display and by the numbers who had wanted to meet the Ark producers. The products sold out, sending a clear message that more could be done. 'We started thinking of doing something important. If there is so much attention, we can do something, we can utilise this attention.' At this point Carlo Petrini took more interest and argued that Slow Food had to work directly with the producers. In 1999 in a meeting in Carlo Petrini's office, Milano, along with Piero Sardo and Paolo di Croce, who had just joined the organisation, heard Petrini instruct them to find 100 Italian Presidia producers for the next Salone, only six months away.

The idea of the Presidia was approved by the Slow Food Trustees. It was nevertheless a significant risk on Slow Food's part; up until then the movement had not had much experience of political economy or any kind of serious collaborations with producers. Moreover, Milano, who was given the job of organising the Presidia, was still without a budget and had few prospects. Frustrated, she nevertheless started to travel to look for possible Presidia products throughout Italy.

The first Presidium product was found in Morozzo, in Piedmont, not far from Bra, where Petrini had attended the festival of the Morozzo Capon, a particular breed of chicken that was facing extinction. The idea of the Presidia had in fact come from a joke of Petrini's that they would need a 'garrison' (the literal meaning of Presidium) to keep globalisation at bay. In the event, after much research, a protocol for Presidia products was developed, according to which they had to meet the criteria of being endangered, having deep historical connections to a place and local identity, and being of distinctive quality. At the Salone del Gusto of 2000, initial fears that nobody would come were again unfounded and, beginning with the strong aroma of the peaches from Leonforte in Sicily, the Presidia producers arrived and there was much publicity in the press.

Slow Food started to receive some generous backing from local regions (notably Tuscany, Piedmont, Veneto, Sicily and Liguria) and there was clear evidence of the possibility of collaboration and wider public interest, though in these pre-Terra Madre days, there was not yet any network to speak of. Petrini, however, was convinced that while the Presidia project had been a success it now had to move beyond Italy. If not, he told his small group of Presidia workers, 'we will remain too provincial and closed. We must open and share information with other countries, including the poorer countries.'

'I was shocked', Milano told me. 'There was no network and no contacts. Above all we had no expertise in poor countries. I was afraid of making mistakes. There were many delicate local contexts. I thought: we have no competence to do this work.' Petrini gave the same answer he always did when eyebrows were raised at one of his suggestions: 'It is not the first time that we have started out on a crazy project.'

The international office, at least, had started to expand, and contacts were improving. In addition Slow Food had received generous backing from a surprising quarter. Following the success of Salone del Gusto in 2000 the agriculture ministry in the incoming Berlusconi government provided 200,000 euros for each Italian Presidium product and the environment ministry had provided funding for an Atlas of all producers in Italian National Parks. This had enabled an office to be set up and had eased the job of trying to locate the potential Presidia producers.

The project of making contact with potential international Presidia producers was as significant for the development of Slow Food in its own way as Terra Madre. It didn't bring people together in one very political environment as Terra Madre was to do, but it did allow Slow Food to map out a distinctive and critical contribution to the political economy of globalisation.

The Foundation has provided Slow Food with some of the practical means of expanding its global network, of bringing together producers, co-producers and academics. It has done this through collaborations on some specific projects. First, the development of the Foundation has provided it with a stronger scientific basis for its work, which has won respect and enabled it to extend its influence. It now has a scientific commission composed of a group of experts responsible for evaluating the Foundation's projects and recommending further initiatives to protect biodiversity. This commission consists of the internationally renowned scientists, Luca Cavalli Sforza, a genetic diversity expert, Marcello Buiatti, another geneticist, who has specialist interests in evolutionary genetics and plant biology, and Vandana Shiva who directs the Research Foundation for Science, Technology and Natural Resource Policy in India and is a 'social ecology' expert. In 1991 she set up Navdanya, an organisation to protect the diversity of native seeds under threat from extinction. Also involved are Aminata Traore, of the African Social Forum and a former Malian Minister of Culture, and Harold McGee, a molecular gastronomy expert, who has produced pioneering works on gastronomic diversity.

Second, the Foundation has worked on common projects alongside other bodies, including social movements, NGOs and supranational institutions. In February 2003, the first meeting was held of the Commission on the Future of Food, set up by Tuscany Regional Authority, which produced a manifesto on food sovereignty to be presented to the World Trade Organisation. Carlo Petrini has said that this was the first time Slow Food had taken part in a collaborative meeting of representatives from environmentalist organisations and that there was an initial suspicion of his gastronomic background – most of the discussion centred on the ecological aspects of industrial agriculture and economic inequality. Petrini's intervention in the meeting, which centred on pleasure as a human right, did not initially dispel the scepticism of the other participants, for whom pleasure was primarily equated with abundance rather than a response to poverty. Petrini's argument was that traditional cultures had strong histories of gastronomic expertise, including in places like India where malnutrition was rife. This knowledge was part of cultural diversity and future prosperity depended on the biodiversity of land and crops. Pleasure, Petrini argued, was prevalent in these traditions and their convivial ways of producing food which had been denied by 'monocultural production'. With the support of Vandana Shiva, whom Petrini first got to know well during this period, he won round other members of the commission. The subsequent *Manifesto on the Future of Food* included the recognition that monocultural production had eroded 'the long celebrated joys of sharing food grown by local hands from local lands'.[11]

This successful intervention by Slow Food, through Petrini's contribution, was significant for its future strategy. It re-positioned the 'politics of pleasure' within a global framework, no longer reduced to the taste buds of Western European gastronomes but extended to the plight of third world producers. It also allowed Slow Food to form meaningful alliances with other organisations.

Other collaborative projects in which Slow Food has been involved include work with the Italian fair trade NGO, CEFA, and Fair Trade Italia on reducing poverty through the promotion of sustainable agriculture and rural development, the promotion of sustainable water and fishing, and work with African food communities in Tanzania. Slow Food has collaborated with the United Nations, through its International Labour Organisation, by using its Presidia work as a way of enhancing local economic development for public bodies and business development. The Slow Food Foundation has contributed to a scheme set up by the Italian Ministry of Agriculture's Co-operation Department which gave emergency help for agricultural reconstruction in the Lebanon in 2006. Working with the Italian NGO, UCODEP, the World Wildlife Fund Italy and the Tuscany Regional Authority, they helped establish farmers' markets to revive local agriculture.

Overall, the Slow Food Foundation has supported an expanding range of initiatives. In 2006 alone, it supported seven major collaborative projects with other institutions. These included the creation of a women's agritourism project in the argan oil production area of Morocco, organised in collaboration with the Piedmont Regional Authority; a project initiated in support of the development of pistachio production in Afghanistan (in collaboration with Italy's Foreign Ministry)

contributed 30,000 euros; collaboration with the Brazilian
Ministry of Agricultural Development helped develop six
Brazilian Presidia, supported by the Veneto Regional Authority
to the tune of 50,000 euros; and the support of four *Mercati
della terra* (literally 'markets of the earth') in Mauritiana,
Lebanon, Bosnia and Croatia, funded by the Tuscany Regional
Authority to the sum of 120,000 euros.

The *Mercati della terra* was a scheme initiated by Slow
Food to support farmers' markets by reducing the chain from
production to the table; that is to cut down on the number of
intermediaries between producers and buyers and to cut down
the distance or 'shopping miles' food travels before it reaches
the consumers. As with other farmers' markets there are the
clear effects of fairer prices for producers and environmental
sustainability. According to Piero Sardo, President of the Slow
Food Foundation for Biodiversity: 'The idea is to set up markets
focused on producers, artisans and small farmers. Local
markets, which are not intended for rural areas but cities.'[12]

The *Mercati della terra* was a network set up in 2006 aimed in
particular at supporting or reviving new markets in developing
countries. It started with the revival of the Missira, the old
artisan market at Bamako, Mali. Here traders and producers
would sell products, including butter, fish and fabrics. The
market had fallen into disrepair and the Slow Food Foundation
has supported the Yeleen association, an initiative started
by Aminata Traore, the former Culture Minister, to restore
the market. Through the Yeleen association, local producers
have worked to revive the market and have provided space
for small farmers to sell their produce, to help set up producer
co-operatives and to restore traditional knowledge through
training younger farmers. The Foundation's grant of 10,000
euros helped to get this project off the ground.

The *Mercati della terra* project was originally conceived at
the University of Gastronomic Sciences, after three students
did a research project on the conditions of farmers' markets

in different parts of the world, visiting markets in the US, UK, Canada, Italy and Ireland. As a result of their research, a criterion of 'good, clean and fair' was developed in consultation with experts, a criteria which Slow Food intends to expand into more farmers' markets. Slow Food has also collaborated on bigger projects. For example, in 2006 it received a grant from the European Union of 223,684 euros for work on raising awareness of biodiversity and in support of sustainable agriculture, promoting and certifying fair trade produce and organising educational activities. It received 378,100 euros from the Italian Foreign Ministry to set up a regional network in support of coffee producers in Central America and the Caribbean. This included the Presidium of Huehuetenango Highlands coffee producers in Guatemala. Under the terms of this project, there were specific 'rules of production' which not only guaranteed quality and respect for the environment but also guidelines on equal status between men and women and equal opportunities to take on leadership roles. Producers who were mothers were allowed an extra 5 per cent on the price of the coffee. There were additional rules on minimum cost and a percentage of the profits were used for 'social utility projects'. This Guatemalan Presidium established a relationship with a prisoners' co-operative in Turin's Vallette prison, whereby Pausa cafe, a social co-operative, works together with prisoners on coffee roasting, receiving coffee from Guatemala at a fair price.

Indeed it is the work of the Slow Food Presidia in developing countries which best illustrates Slow Food's idea of virtuous globalisation. In Italy, where the Presidia first started and where there is an older Slow Food network, there are nearly 200 Presidia projects. By 2008 there were 105 Presidia projects in 43 countries outside Italy. Of these there were 29 in Latin America, 8 in Africa, 6 in Asia (including one each in India, China and Afghanistan) and 11 in Eastern Europe. Considering there were 5 in the US, 6 in the UK and 1 in Germany, this represents a significant shift in the priorities and work of Slow Food, since the setting up of the Foundation in 2003 and the development of the international Presidia.

Research published in 2002 by the Italian daily business newspaper *Il Sole 24 Ore* proposed an evaluation of the economic results of the Italian Presidia. Slow Food agreed and worked with *Il Sole* and the Bocconi University in Milan. The results of research into 54 Italian Presidia projects showed a significant rise in sales and price rises for the producers. In 2006, Slow Food repeated the exercise in a much wider and more comprehensive in-depth study of 35 Presidia products from across the world. In addition to the economic benefits there were significant environmental and social effects arising from the Presidia projects.[13]

The idea of virtuous globalisation is reflected through the Presidia's work in sustaining local identity and culture in the face of the neo-liberal global market. This is therefore not only about preserving foods that are at risk but also about articulating a distinctive 'sense of place' within a global context. A key aspect of this is the strong emphasis on diversity, which contrasts sharply with the homogenising tendencies of neo-liberal globalisation: a recognition that an alternative idea of globalisation has to be reflected through diverse cultural experiences. For Carlo Petrini, this became apparent in his travels with Slow Food, where amongst others he has encountered the Sami community in Sweden (sometimes called 'Laplanders', though this is regarded as offensive by the community themselves). This is a population of 70,000 people located in northern Scandinavia. They are a nomadic community and in 2004 a group attended Terra Madre as one of the food communities. This food community worked with the herds of reindeer they followed and from which they made *suovas*, smoked reindeer meat. In November 2004, Carlo Petrini visited the Sami food community, and was guided by the president of the Sami parliament. He heard the story of the injustices they faced, the problems they encountered in enforcing their right to travel, and their pride in their nomadic identity which had survived the pressures of modern Scandinavian life. He was told that they had been inspired by Terra Madre and it had helped set up a kind of network, allowing them to keep in touch with Mongolian shepherds over the Internet. For Petrini this was further evidence that modern communications can work with traditional culture in the Slow Food network and that the involvement of indigenous communities (which has also included Native Americans amongst its activists in the US) gives further practical meaning to Slow Food's commitment to diversity and local identity:

> It is therefore not utopian to think that the various modern means of communication can be put at the service of this idea [of the network]; indeed, the example of the Sami and the Mongolians may be a practical demonstration of a new way of circulating ideas and giving self-respect to these peoples, who stoically survive in lands where it is truly difficult to live.[14]

Slow Food's idea of virtuous globalisation illustrates a way in which *difference*, through people's relationship to food, can enhance common life in a more interdependent way. This allows it to address some of the most important questions of contemporary living, such as, in the cultural theorist Stuart Hall's formulation:

> How are people from different cultures, different backgrounds, with different languages, different religious beliefs, produced by different and highly uneven histories, but who find themselves either directly connected because they've got to make a life together in the same place, or digitally connected because they occupy the same symbolic worlds - how are they to make some sort of common life together without retreating into warring tribes, eating one another, or insisting that other people must look exactly like you, behave exactly like you, think exactly like you - that is to say cultural assimilation? How can we recognise the true, real, complicated diversity of the planet - societies produced by different forms of development, etc., which is what constitutes

difference? Different histories, different cultures, over long periods of time, have produced a variegated world, but the barriers are now breaking down. People find themselves obliged to make a common life or at least find some common ground of negotiation.[15]

Slow Food's cultural politics has opened up a new debate on the future of food. In doing so, it has revisited at a broader level the important questions of our time, notably the relationship between producers and consumers, the connections between local and global places, the significance of identity, culture and difference, and the dialectic of political and social change.

9

Slow Food, Gastronomy and Cultural Politics

FOOD NOW DOMINATES the political agendas of many Western countries. Government policies on curbing obesity, concern over factory farming and the costs of maltreatment of animals, mounting 'food miles' of the increasingly diverse items sold throughout the year in multinational supermarkets, as well as a rising number of alternative consumption movements and the desire for local produce and farmers' markets, have combined to tax the minds of both politicians and activists. If we add the questions of famine and fair trade, then food becomes one of the most contested sites in contemporary politics, offering a distinctive 'way in' to critical discussions over the nature of globalisation and the burning human questions of our time.

This growing breadth of food issues has precipitated a variety of responses, from governments, NGOs, celebrity gourmets, health experts, scientists and environmentalists. The urgency now given to obesity and famine has been matched in its intensity by the bewildering variety of explanations, studies and policy initiatives, many of which have contradictory findings and proposals. Food has become the archetypal example of that 'postmodern ambivalence' where our attitudes to living are no longer governed by the same certainties about health and quality of life because many of the scientific frameworks have broken down. Experts have lost authority – in the cases of BSE, GM food and nutrition – while, on the other hand, more 'reflexive' individuals exercise greater autonomy in making choices on how to live. As a result, although the routes to the good life are now crowded with obstacles and confusions, individuals have shown a greater propensity to exercise more control over their lives.

The new politics of food has driven a range of responses, from self-help groups to boycotts, educational initiatives, voluminous newspaper articles and new areas of research across a range of academic disciplines. It has also led to a new type of contrarian politics, with different faultlines than before: pro- and anti- positions on school dinner strategies, dieting and shopping, and campaigns to tackle obesity, some of which cut across traditional ideological boundaries. Thus some left-wing British socialists, for example, side with neo-liberals in resisting what they see as 'food fascism', whereby people are sharply rebuked for eating the 'wrong' foods, while discussions of the pleasures of food and eating well are regarded with the suspicion normally found amongst catholic conservatives. Some British conservatives, on the other hand, share with environmentalists a desire for stronger stewardship of the natural landscape. American farmers in Iowa have more in common than they might think with green socialists in Berlin in seeking to alter the course of modern agricultural policy. In food, which has become the terrain where some of the biggest global political issues of our time are fought out, ideological boundaries have become less fixed and predictable.

As a consequence, while the social movements which have grown around food in recent years reflect some of the features of the earlier movements of the 1960s and 1970s, there are significant differences. The similarities lie in the ways in which the meaning of politics has to be extended to the areas of personal choice and lifestyle, including, in the case of ethical consumption, new identities around sustainable food shopping. As Roberta Sassatelli has put it:

For a long time consumption was mainly described as a private act, untouched by power: aligned with the market, commerce, the family and pushed into the private sphere, consumption was opposed to the public and political spheres of the state, of citizenship and rights. However, it is becoming increasingly evident that both the ways in which consumption is represented and the ways in which it is carried out are deeply intertwined with power relationships.[1]

There is also a stronger sense of the autonomy of social movements as a channel of political agency. The feelings of empowerment through collective action, particularly in the assertion of particular identities, has become more marked. The differences relate to the weakening of class as an organising frame for political action in the shifts towards a 'post-materialist' politics. However, paradoxically, the centrality of globalisation, another key difference from the earlier decades, has reinforced forms of class politics at a further global level. Indeed the key difference between the new movements which emerged in the 1990s and those of earlier decades lies in their global configuration, with the real possibility of organising alternative global networks and forms of solidarity.

The main continuity between the contemporary movements that have formed around food and those of the 1960s and 1970s can be found in the more expansive view of politics, one which recognises the importance and centrality of culture and which sees the private, personal and local as sites of political struggle. This view of politics has many influences, including the formative era of the New Left, but was first elaborated by Antonio Gramsci, in his prison writings in the 1920s and 1930s, and subsequently mediated by a mixture of historians, political figures and Western intellectuals. Gramsci wanted to move away from the economism which assumed that political and social change would follow economic transformation, whereby culture is relegated to a peripheral or dependent variable – an appendage, if you like, to the more fundamental economic structure. Gramsci's view, which later influenced a new generation of political activists, intellectuals and 'cultural studies' academics, was that to understand the dynamics of social change we needed to *know* empirically the 'ways of living' of a particular people, including their beliefs, traditions and fragmentary knowledges, folklore and common sense.

Indeed, a not insignificant part of Gramsci's Prison Notebooks and cultural writings includes extended discussions of popular culture and literature, as well as a rich insight into Italian social and cultural history. This priority of 'knowing' a culture influenced writers and film directors such as Pier Paolo Pasolini, who immersed himself in the language and ways of life of the Roman underclass, in movies like *Accattone*.

The shift initiated by Gramsci has had a profound impact on the meaning of politics, with culture now a key terrain of political struggle. For the cultural theorist Stuart Hall, culture is 'constitutive' in that it has provided the values, beliefs, symbolic meanings and identities which contain real power and thus have a major bearing on politics. They provide political actors with the resources for political interventions. In recent times the growth of cultural industries and globalisation have combined to create new imaginary worlds and symbolic meanings, all of which become political in their relationship to power, either by helping legitimise existing socio-economic structures or in challenging them. Culture can also represent different ways of life: a rural or urban existence, a particular type of mainstream 'American' way of living or the Italian slow lifestyle, have become more sharply focused in the minds of people as a result.

As far as food is concerned, the cultural terrain is rich in sites of political struggle, from the defence of the diversity of local food in response to the monocultures of globalisation to the symbolic protests of consumer movements in conflict with large corporations. The Slow Food movement has provided a further illustration of this kind of cultural politics. With its origins in the movements of the 1960s and 1970s, and the continuing resonance of the key ideas of that decade, it has become a modern exponent, if an unlikely one, of a distinctive kind of cultural politics. Part of its distinctiveness lies in its commitment to aesthetic pleasure, where sensual experience, taste and concern for the preparation of food are important. In this way Slow Food shares similarities with other art forms. Thomas Struck, a German film director has organised the 'Culinary Cinema' strand at the Berlin Film Festival since 2007: a mixture of screenings, talks and dinners. According to Struck, whom I met in Berlin in late 2007, there are some sharp comparisons to be made between film and food cultures, which Slow Food has been keen to develop. 'Through film, Slow Food has the power to rejuvenate people, otherwise it will be a tasting club of the elderly.' He finds links between Slow Food's desire to 'be authentic, to be true to yourself' and that of the artist in general:

> By going deeper into food, you will be going deeper into the feelings about your culture. Timing is crucial for both, necessary in the basic talent for cooking as well as making films. Making food and making films are much closer to each other than people are aware of. When you start it is because something has inspired you. All film parts are ingredients and have long stories. This wine comes from a region with a particular history. It is the same with films. Stories are rooted, we need to think of roots, to get to the essence of things. The period of pre-production is as important to food as it is for film.
>
> Now comes the moment to turn on a camera, or open the oven when you turn on the heat. Focus the camera and start the oven. ... There are really deep connections between the two. Food goes right back to the beginning of civilisation when we needed to tame the fire for a hot meal. Film is also at the beginning of a new civilisation, a new way of communicating. Now they have come together.

The 'Culinary Cinema' strand of the 2008 Festival also included 'A Day in Eataly', a documentary of Slow Food's first supermarket which opened in Turin in 2007, that Struck made with the cinematographer Michael Ballhaus, with the help of students at the University of Gastronomic Sciences. Further collaboration between Struck, his colleagues and the University students enabled the latter to make video documentaries of their own research as they travelled different regions and countries of the world. Their use of film has also helped keep alive particular species at risk and the different ways of preparing food, and this work has formed the basis of a research database. Another Slow Food film, 'Mr Bene Goes to Italy', a story of a Terra Madre delegate's visit to Turin, was also shown at Berlin in 2008.

Slow Food has held its own annual film festival, originally in Bra but from 2008 in Bologna, organised in collaboration with *Cineteca Bologna*. Its founding objective, according to the Slow Food website, was the promotion of

a new critical awareness of food culture through the screening of films, short films, documentaries and TV series that focus on food-related issues (drives, perversions, identity and emotional implications) in an original way as well as on the agricultural and food industry's repercussions on society and the environment and on gastronomic memory as a common heritage to be safeguarded.

The question of taste provides more illumination on the distinctive cultural politics of Slow Food. Pierre Bourdieu found food to be one of the key aspects of 'distinction' between French social classes in the development and maintenance of the social structure in France. Bourdieu found that tastes were 'markers' of class, and distinguished between what he called a 'taste of necessity', defined by economic circumstance, and a 'taste of luxury', where the emphasis is on the presentation of the food and stylistic nuances:

The denial of lower, coarse, vulgar, venal, servile – in a word, natural – enjoyment which constitutes the sacred sphere of culture, implies an affirmation of the superiority of those who can be satisfied with the sublimated, refined, disinterested, gratuitous, distinguished pleasures forever closed to the profane. That is why art and cultural consumption are predisposed, consciously and deliberately or not, to fulfil a social function of legitimating social differences.[2]

Bourdieu found that there were class differences involved, such as that between 'working-class conviviality', where the local café was a place of 'companionship', and the more formal 'refined' circumstances in which the bourgeoisie would eat, shunning the 'free and easy' habits of the manual workers. Drawing on research in the 1970s, he found that the skilled manual workers spent more of their income on food, particularly on wine, foie gras and game, while middle-class employees ate more sparingly, concerned with 'healthier' choices.[3]

A comparison of Bourdieu's analysis with Slow Food's approach reveals some interesting connections. First, the 'working-class conviviality' he describes is very similar to Slow Food's celebration of the conviviality of the local osteria, while confirming the strong place of food in the cultures of ordinary French and Italians. Second, Bourdieu's emphasis on taste as a social construction whereby different aesthetic choices are 'distinctions', made to contrast with the choices of other social classes, carries a different emphasis from Slow Food which believes taste can be assessed scientifically. Indeed, Slow Food offers courses in taste education, while the University of Gastronomic Sciences runs courses on sensory analysis as part of its degree programme. Taste becomes political in Slow Food's argument because of the effect standardisation has had on the palates of ordinary people. There is a recognition however that cultural diversity is crucial in deciding taste preferences and choices.

Slow Food's aesthetic considerations are probably the reason why the role food plays in the development of cultural identity and diversity, for example, has received less attention in cultural studies than, say, the relationship between identity and fashion, music, or sport, or attitudes towards sexuality. This seems to reflect a northern European bias in cultural studies which has less interest in food, confirmed by the numbers of journals and space given to other issues, though food has been discussed more widely in social anthropology and environmental studies. It certainly reflects the view that discussions of food are inevitably framed by 'elitist' assumptions, perhaps because of this emphasis on aesthetic pleasure. Some have suggested that this is due to a general shift towards populist or relativist assumptions which see no useful difference between aesthetic culture – based on quality, excellence and taste – and mainstream culture. This has even led some to predict the death of high culture.

Much of the limited coverage that has been given to Slow Food within cultural studies has been shaped by these and related assumptions. Critics point to the 'elite' nature of Slow Food's membership, its 'nostalgic' view of the past, its 'fetishised' view of pleasure, its 'paternalism', its 'imperial encounters' with its 'exoticised others' (framed by its own 'heritage of privilege'), and its 'culinary Luddism'. Slow Food members, according to critics, are an 'upper-middle-class' elite, able to partake in events, such as dinners, that are out of the economic reach of ordinary people. It is not only the costs of the events that make Slow Food an elite organisation, it is argued, but the lifestyles and occupations of the members which give them the opportunity to indulge in luxuries, make distinctions on grounds of taste, and enjoy the benefits of local produce while ordinary people are restricted to the cheaper supermarket chains.[4]

These arguments are difficult to substantiate when applied to the Slow Food movement of 2008. Above all, such arguments underestimate the *politics* of Slow Food. From its political origins in Italy, to its elaborate critique of global inequality, and Terra Madre, it would be inaccurate to depict the movement any longer as a gastronomic elite. Certainly there is no doubt that Slow Food members in the Western convivia are drawn disproportionately from middle-class professions, but this is not surprising in itself, since many other social movements – including the Campaign for Nuclear Disarmament, and many civil rights and environmentalist movements – have had a similar social composition, particularly in their formative years. The counter-cultural movements of the 1960s were also disproportionately composed of middle-class students and academics. There is a difficulty in how far one takes this as indicative of 'elitist values' (cultural studies academics are also predominantly middle class), when many movements are led or initiated by an enlightened or 'reflexive' middle class, to use Paul Ginsborg's phrase.[5] It is not difficult to argue that the ideas of the 1960s, such as egalitarian attitudes and personal freedoms, have become more mainstream in contemporary societies; the big increase in organic and ethical consumption, and the greater awareness of the origins of food, now supported by a range of evidence, suggest that a similar pattern of enlightenment is emerging amongst contemporary movements.

The discussion about class amongst some of the Slow Food critics is fraught with confusion. Some of the typical representations of this elitism of Slow Food members, for example of a 'well-heeled, wine-sipping Slow Food elite who have the good fortune of opting in or out of the global food supply',[6] make all kinds of assumptions about social status and use very unreliable ('wine-sipping') criteria of social class that cannot be applied to the Slow Food membership at large, given the different food cultures. Such arguments often seem oblivious to the wider global economy. How can a debate about class, for example, be conducted primarily around whether one shops at Tesco or Waitrose (to give a British example) when the cheap produce provided by mass supermarkets is guaranteed by exploitative labour in developing countries? It is surely absurd to restrict discussions of the *class* politics of food to whether people are consumers of supermarket food or local producers, without an understanding of the global economic pressures which make cheap produce available at supermarkets on the back of poverty wages in the third world. One of the contributions of Slow Food, along with other movements, has been to help further the debate on the precarious class positions of small producers in the South.

Indeed it is noticeable that much of the criticism of Slow Food's 'elitism' is driven by a particular notion of social status that carries particular cultural meanings. But the structural economic context is still imperative when considering these questions at a global level. Analysis of Slow Food documents, or its leaders' speeches and projects, demonstrates that the recurrent global economic and environmental crisis is pivotal. As I pointed out in Chapter 2, there is a wealth of evidence which demonstrates that people of all social classes spend a significantly less proportion of their income on food than in the past, while also spending more on other consumer items such as computer games or satellite TV. These spending variations are of course the outcome of cultural choices, but, significant inequalities in income notwithstanding, they should not be confused with economic constraints.

Nor is it the case that there is a clear 'class' perspective of Slow Food members which directs 'elitist' attitudes towards the behaviours and values of the 'lower classes'. It is true that its membership includes food writers and restaurateurs – if you like, the 'opinion-formers' of the food agenda – but this might also be testimony to the growing strength and influence of its philosophy. Slow Food has not noticeably compromised its politics and much of its main critique is directed towards the homogenised, standardised cultures of corporate capitalism. In fact it is the habits and values – at times the superficiality and 'vulgarity' – of *corporate* culture, including its service ethic, its indifference to taste, and its unthinking association of wealth with value, that is often a target of Slow Food criticism.

This is less an elitist judgment of the poor than the view that the bourgeoisie, as Marx argued in the *Critique of the Gotha Programme*, is in need of a 'stern education by the people'. Slow Food activists often told me how odd they find it that shopping at local places in danger of going out of business attracts the elitist label, while shopping at multi-nationals which are able to keep prices down because of exploitative wages, to say nothing of the associated environmental damage, is regarded more favourably by some. This is reflected in a backlash from some sectors of the liberal press to Slow Food and the ethical consumption movement where the supermarket has been defended against 'noisy self-satisfied oppositionists', as the *Observer* food and restaurant critic described those who supported attempts to regulate supermarket competition in the UK.[7] Elsewhere, Jamie Oliver's plea for consumers to spend a bit extra on free range chickens instead of battery hens was dismissed as a 'rich person demanding impoverishing consumer choices from a poorer person'.[8]

The nostalgic view of the past as some kind of rural idyll is certainly held by parts of the Slow Food membership, and I found that the representation of Italy as 'an imagined slow community' betrayed some of these assumptions. However it is difficult to accept that this is the mainstream view of the Slow Food leaders, who in interviews have generally gone to some pains to deny simplistic views of the past; likewise the official documents related to traditional Slow Food produce, which have increasingly been subject to quite rigorous scientific criteria as well as oral testimonies from local people. The ideologies of all movements contain mythical elements, whether it is the idealised nuclear family in the conservative view, or an egalitarian paradise envisaged by socialists of the 1970s.

Many of the criticisms of Slow Food's engagement with small producers in third world countries – their 'exotic other' – were made before Terra Madre and the development of projects involving producers. Then it was easier to categorise Slow Food as a mainly Western consumer organisation. Slow Food has also been accused of paternalism in its links with producers, yet its initiatives are focused primarily on support for local economic revival rather than aid, and are driven by a sharp critique of the inequities of the global system. Unlike some other NGOs and movements that are restricted to acting on behalf of, or in empathy with, small producers, Slow Food has offered them greater autonomy as well as investment in enabling them to travel and, in some cases, to promote and help sustain their local businesses.

It is the pleasure factor which has given rise to confusion in the intersections between class, food and elitism in Slow Food's distinctive cultural politics. It is true that aesthetic pleasure remains crucial to Slow Food's values, but it is the link between pleasure and responsibility that defines its politics. Wine and food tasting remains the 'staple diet' of most convivium events, but they are often more than this, combining speeches, themes or a focus on foods at risk, or presenting local producers in economic difficulty. This is apparent in the vibrant London convivium, which organises an intense schedule of events. In a space of a couple of months between December 2007 and February 2008, there were events on 'comparative spice tasting', an evening with the food writer Michael Pollan, the 'A–Z of lesser grape varieties', 'a culinary tour of East Dulwich', and a Terra Madre dinner. The latter event, held at the Duke of Cambridge, a renowned 'gastro pub' in Islington, north London, introduced some lesser known wines from Emilia Romagna, donated the proceeds of the dinner to the Gabon development fund, and accommodated a couple of powerful political speeches between courses. In one of these, Patrick Mulvany, chair of the UK Food Group, the main network of British NGOs working in the area of food, delivered a strong speech on the need for food sovereignty in Africa. He argued that, free of colonialism and globalisation, Africa 'can feed itself', echoing the slogan of the 'Forum for Food Sovereignty', held earlier in 2007 in Mali, which had brought together 500 people from 80 countries, including farmers, indigenous peoples, environmentalists and people working in NGOs. His argument that food sovereignty was an issue for all countries and peoples, and depended on a struggle for social justice against 'corporate, industrialised food systems', evidently roused the diners.

The Slow Food movement has helped generate a broader theoretical perspective which has begun to influence thinking on a range of issues, from local government strategy to quality of life issues. This emerging *slow theory* amounts to a critical, theoretical engagement with globalisation. It primarily challenges the assumption that the dogma of speed is the only way to guarantee economic efficiency and social well-being. It gives some meaning to what is missing from this equation, namely lost pleasures and redundant knowledges, the costs and consequences of globalisation for the environment and biodiversity. According to Nicola Perullo, Professor of Aesthetics at the University of Gastronomic Sciences, we should now talk of 'slow knowledge' which in its emphasis on wisdom, understanding and experience, offers a counter to that 'fast knowledge' which has become reduced to technologically driven information that 'can easily be reproduced and applied elsewhere':

> From a *fast* perspective, knowing means absorbing limitless masses of information, a sort of supermarket of thought, aiming to enable us to definitively overcome our ignorance and that part of 'mystery' which surrounds human life. According to the *slow* model however, human beings, since they are finite and mortal, are incomplete and structurally imperfect; more precisely, they are part of nature and not its absolute master. ... Slow vision ... loosens and weakens the constricting mesh of technocratic and economistic rationality. It makes us take responsibility for ourselves and our community, driven not by the death instinct (the true origin of the deplorable ideology of profit and competition, the bringer of defeat and

anxiety), but by the principle of pleasure, enjoyment and joy in the 'perfection' of our finite and imperfect human condition.[9]

Slow theory offers a new set of values for 'slow living', what Parkins and Craig call 'a new form of being in the world'. As an emerging theoretical perspective, it offers new insight on such questions as identity and cultural difference, and a re-evaluation of the local–global interconnections. The issues it raises for identity are rooted in the importance of place, and the commitment to territory, but also in the way in which traditional crafts and skills in the production of food have defined a person's place in the world. Identities have become stronger in the assertion of local culture and trade in the face of global, economic and technological changes. The mutual understandings between producers from different countries both illustrate and reinforce these identities while also pointing to the importance of cultural diversity in the way in which identity is expressed and maintained.

The Slow Food emphasis on cultural diversity is evident in many ways and far more complex than is usually recognised. First, the commitment to biodiversity is not only an ecological necessity but a positive endorsement of the value of diverse tastes, traditions and agricultural methods. Second, cultural diversity stands in opposition to the monocultures of multi-national corporations and industrial agriculture. Cultural diversity asserts 'local' difference within a global framework, including the trajectory towards re-localisation. Cultural difference is also expressed within localities between different ethnic or cultural groupings, as we have seen through the Sami community, or ethnic food communities in large metropolises like San Francisco and London.

Slow Food's cultural politics is also distinguished by a distinctive political language, the depth and extent of which has generated a dictionary of terms.[10] The leading concepts such as 'co-producer', the 'dialogue of realms', 'virtuous globalisation', as well as eco-gastronomy itself, have delineated Slow Food's politics. They have helped to clarify its political positions, articulate distinctive political meanings, and usefully set out its ideology of change. The use of the term 'co-producer' has given it a distinctive interpretation of the effects of consumerism in an age of abundance. Petrini has problematised the use of the term consumption, for two related reasons. First, he argues that the real meaning of consumption – 'wearing out, using up, destroying, progressively exhausting'[11] – has been disguised in the positive celebration of the term in everyday language. This has made the task of warning against the environmental damage of over-consumption and waste of resources much more difficult. Second, he argues that the consumer must come to feel closer to the production process, rather than separate from it as an isolated free-floating individual. This view of consumption has been seen by some as indicative of the culture of modern capitalism, summed up in Zygmunt Bauman's phrase 'liquid modernity' which, with its atomised view of the individual and the erosion of traditional experiences and skills under pressure of the knowledge economy, invokes Marx's view of the expansion of global capitalism where 'all that is solid melts into air'. The commodification of virtually all aspects of social life has left a fractured society devoid of meaning other than monetary value and incapable of reviving forms of common life. As Jonathan Rutherford argues:

> Consumer culture and its tantalising promises offers a panacea to fend off ... uncertainty. But its effects can be corrosive, because it reconstitutes social activities and relations between people as market relations between individuals and things. The process of commodification leads to an isolating world inhabited by men and women whose social bonds are displaced or depleted. Like shoppers hunting for a bargain, we do not want to be distracted from pursuing our own elusive desire, splitting it off from our emotional need and our dependence on others. Desire is the idiom of our aliveness, but desire without a qualifying and balancing attachment to others casts us into a pursuit of the unattainable.

Hovering in the wings are the new social threats of invisibility, meaningless, failure.[12]

The focus on the 'co-producer' also attempts to redress the balance between traditional skills and modern knowledge eroded in a society driven by multi-skilling, deskilling and downsizing. This has serious implications for the traditional artisan skills. As the distinguished sociologist Richard Sennett argues in *The Culture of the New Capitalism*:

> The emerging social order militates against the ideal of craftsmanship, that is, learning to do just one thing really well; such commitment can often prove economically destructive. In place of craftsmanship, modern culture advances an idea of meritocracy which celebrates potential ability rather than past achievement.[13]

His following book, *The Craftsman*, contains the argument that 'anyone can become a good craftsman'.[14] This view has become heretical because of the way people are now stratified strictly on grounds of perceived notions of ability. It prioritises one kind of knowledge, if you like the 'work, talent, consumption', the so-called 'skills society' in which 'jobs in the old sense of random movement now prevail; people are meant to deploy a portfolio of skills rather than nurture a single ability in the course of their working histories; this succession of projects or tasks erodes belief that one is meant to do just one thing well'.[15] However Sennett rejects the view that craftsmanship was made redundant by industrialisation and predicts a future in which the 'craft habit and material focus' learned by artisanal craftsman will once again become important in retraining and instilling a 'sense of vocation'.

A similar view underpins Slow Food's concept of the 'dialogue of realms', its succinct attempt to explain the relevance of different forms of knowledge in addressing the ambiguities of an uncertain age. Slow Food is not against new forms of knowledge but questions the erosion of traditional knowledge, arguing that the cultural heritage of farmers and local food cultures needs to be preserved. Through the University of Gastronomic Sciences and other projects they have encouraged collaboration between scientists and producers, for example between agro-ecology and traditional knowledge. Slow Food's view is that both realms now share equal authority and they deserve equal respect.

Virtuous globalisation encompasses Slow Food's critical interpretation of the contemporary agenda, while articulating an alternative which goes beyond mere opposition and has provided another distinctive voice to a growing consensus that a global system which recognises biodiversity – and the capacity of poorer countries in the South to feed themselves given the chance to develop their local economies – can be made to work. Slow Food's projects, the Presidia and the work of the Slow Food Foundation for Biodiversity, provide some concrete examples of this. Slow Food, which in part owes its origin to the counter-culture, can perhaps now be seen – as Eleanor Bertino, a contemporary of Alice Waters now working in food public relations, told me in San Francisco – as part of a 'parallel culture'. This parallel culture consists of a set of contrasting ecological and economic values, evident, at one level, in the work on the ground with small producers. At another level, the parallel culture can be seen to have developed, in embryo, more interdependent socio-economic relations between 'local' and 'global' places. In what I have described as its pre-figurative philosophy, Slow Food has made an important start in articulating through its public discourse and events, as well as through its concrete initiatives, an alternative way of living.

It is, though, the idea of eco-gastronomy that will determine Slow Food's future. This could be one of the leading ideas of the next decades. Gastronomy, which incorporates everything that concerns the preparation, production and consumption of food, has made a dramatic re-appearance in the era of globalisation. The new gastronomy, which has found converts amongst

Western consumers aspiring to a better quality of life, has also emerged as an academic discipline, with a new international university, new food studies centres, and the presence of eco-gastronomy on the curriculum. More widely, it has resulted in an unlikely new political subject, the gastronome, reflected above all in the personality of its leading figure. A modern mixture of Jean Anthelme Brillat-Savarin and William Morris, Carlo Petrini has seen the movement which started out from his home town of Bra, on the back of the dreamy idealism of the 1970s, make the unique, but now crucial, connection between the future of the planet and the desires of the palate. Eating is not only 'an agricultural act', it is also a 'cultural act', and the political and pleasurable ramifications of this are deep and far-reaching.

List of Osterias and Restaurants

A Cannata, Salina, Italy
Alstadt, Brasov, Romania
Ancora, Krakow, Poland
Antica Focacceria San Francesco, Palermo, Sicily
Budellino, Bra, Italy
Balthazar, New York
Bataglino, Bra, Italy
Café Donizetti, Bergamo, Italy
Caminetto D'Oro, Bologna, Italy
Cantina Bentivoglio, Bologna, Italy
Casa Cu Cerb, Sighisoara, Romania
Chez Panisse, Berkeley, California
Cucina & Vino, Ragusa Ibla, Sicily
Da Tonino, Rome
Duke of Cambridge, London
Gramercy Tavern, New York
Hotel Belvair, Zuoz, Switzerland
Jardin de las Trinitarias, Puebla, Mexico
Konstam, London
La Fraschetta, Rome
Luther & Wegner, Berlin
Mesun Bilbao, London
Metro, Catania, Sicily
Musco de San Pedro, Puebla, Mexico
Osteria Murivecchi, Bra, Italy
Osteria Boccondivino, Bra, Italy
Osteria dell'Arco, Alba, Italy
Osteria La Torre, Cherasco, Italy
Osteria Le Torre, Castiglione Falletto, Italy
Out the Door, San Francisco, California
Porto Bello, Salina, Italy
Roast, Borough Market, London
Sant Andrea, Palermo, Sicily
Sokolowski's University Inn, Cleveland, Ohio
Sora Margherita, Rome
SPQR, San Francisco, California
The Breakfast Club, Chicago
The Clive, Ludlow, UK
Trattoria Fantoni, Bologna, Italy
Trattoria Primavera, Palermo, Sicily

Notes

Chapter 1

1. S. Rizzo and G.A. Stella, *La Casta* (Rizzoli 2007).
2. For an excellent account of these years see C. Petrini and G. Padovani, *Slow Food Revolution* (Rizzoli International 2006). I am also grateful to Azio Citi and Carlo Petrini for their recollections in interviews.
3. Ibid., pp. 32–9.
4. 'Associazione degli amici del Barolo'. See ibid., p. 24.
5. Ibid., p. 12.
6. T. McNamee, *Alice Waters and Chez Panisse: The Romantic, Impractical, Often Eccentric, Ultimately Brilliant Making of a Food Revolution* (Penguin 2007), p. 39.
7. Ibid., p. 45.
8. A thought-provoking account of the origins of Chez Panisse and the career of Alice Waters can be found in David Kamp, 'Cooking Up a Storm', *Vanity Fair*, October 2006.
9. Interview with author. Pollan, dressed in a 'Vote With Your Fork' T-shirt, was in London at the time of our interview to promote his bestselling book, *In Defence of Food*.
10. Interview with author. See also Warren Belasco, *Appetite For Change: How the Counter-Culture Took on the Food Industry* (2nd edn, Cornell University Press 2006).
11. McNamee, *Alice Waters and Chez Panisse*, p. xiii.
12. J. Dickie, *Delizia* (Hodder and Stoughton 2007).
13. Quoted in P. Freedman (ed.), *Food: The History of Taste* (University of California Press 2007), pp. 265–6.
14. C. Petrini, *Slow Food Nation: Why Our Food Should Be Good, Clean and Fair* (Rizzoli International 2007), p. 44.
15. V. Shiva, *Dalla Parte Degli Ultimi: Una vita per I diritti dei contadini* (Slow Food Editore 2007).
16. C. Petrini, *Slow Food: The Case For Taste* (Columbia University Press 2003), pp. 102–3.
17. W. Parkins and G. Craig, *Slow Living* (Berg 2006), p. 124.
18. Petrini has said this in several different places, including in his speech at the Royal Society for the Arts, London, 8 June 2007.
19. B. Wilson, 'What Makes a Pig Organic?', *Financial Times*, 12 January 2007.
20. M. Fort, 'Tradition of Innovation', *Slow*, April 2005, pp. 66–9.

21. M. Montanari, *Food is Culture* (Columbia University Press 2006), p. 7.

22. R. Reeves, 'Middle England: They're Nicer Than You Think', *New Statesman*, 25 October 2007.

23. Carlo Petrini recounts this meeting in an article for *La Repubblica* 'Carlo d'Inghilterra: un manifesto per la terra', 16 December 2007.

24. Michael Pollan, *In Defence of Food* (Allen Lane 2008).

25. See interviews in *La Stampa*, 27 May 2007, *Corriere della Sera*, 31 May 2007 and 2 June 2007. Also C. Petrini interview with author.

Chapter 2

1. Petrini in conversation with Padovani, *Slow Food Revolution*, p. 71.

2. Ibid., pp. 71–2.

3. J. Gleick, *Faster: The Acceleration of Just About Everything* (Pantheon 1999).

4. C. Honoré, *In Praise of Slow* (Orion 2004), p. 14.

5. Ibid., pp. 4–5.

6. M. Castells, *The Information Age, Vol. I: The Rise of the Network Society* (Blackwell 2000), p. 466.

7. Ibid., p. 473.

8. Ibid., p. 497.

9. M. Castells, *The Information Age, Vol. II: The Power of Identity* (Blackwell 2004), p. 2.

10. C. Leadbeater, *Living on Thin Air* (Penguin 1999), p. 3.

11. Ibid., p. 7.

12. Ibid., p. 13.

13. Ibid., p. 233.

14. Belknap Press of Harvard University Press 2005.

15. Ibid., p. 12.

16. G. Ritzer, 'The Globalization of Nothing', *Slow*, April 2005, p. 28.

17. Ibid., p. 30.

18. Eric Schlosser, *Fast Food Nation* (Harper Perennial 2005), p. 3.

19. Joanna Blythman, *Shopped: The Shocking Power of British Supermarkets* (Fourth Estate London 2004), p. xi.

20. Blythman's statistics are based on the *Department of the Environment, Transport and the Regions* survey of foodstores and statistics compiled by the Meat and Livestock Commission.

21. Ibid., p. 9. See also A. Simms, *Tescopoly* (Constable 2007) and the unrelated campaigning organisation of the same name: www.tescopoly.org

22. As the Terra Madre newsletter of January 2008 points out.
23. Petrini, *Slow Food Nation*, p. 180.
24. *Cittaslow: progetto per una citta del buon vivere* (2002).
25. Parkins and Craig, *Slow Living*, Preface.
26. Ibid., p. 1.
27. For an excellent discussion of these issues see Roberta Sassatelli, 'Critical Consumerism: Virtue, Responsibility and Consumer Choice', in J. Brewer and F. Trentmann (eds), *Consuming Cultures* (Berg 2006), pp. 219–50.
28. R. Sassatelli, 'The Political Morality of Food', in M. Harvey and A. Warde, *Qualities of Food* (Manchester University Press 2004), p. 363.
29. See US Centers for Disease Control and Prevention Report 2005 and the ESRC Report in 2007 on 'Diet and Obesity in UK': www.esrcsocietytoday.co.uk
30. P. Martins and B. Watson, *The Slow Food Guide to New York City* (Chelsea Green Publishing 2003).
31. See M. Plant and M. Plant, *Binge Britain* (Open University Press 2006).
32. *British Behaviour Abroad*, Foreign and Commonwealth Office 2007, reports the experiences of the British Embassy in Prague of having to deal with frequent cases of drunkenness. In addition, the Czech Republic, Tallinn, Bratislava, Riga and Krakow were popular destinations for stag and hen parties.
33. Julie Burchill, 'Lights, Action, Thrills: I Love my Weekly Romance with Tesco', *The Times*, 8 October 2005.
34. Research on spending on food as a percentage of income is available from the US Department of Agriculture: www.ers.usda.gov/publications; for similar figures on the UK see the Food Standards agency report at www.food.gov.uk
35. P. Bourdieu, *Distinction* (Blackwell 1984).
36. Dickie, *Delizia*, p. 345.

Chapter 3

1. Petrini and Padovani, *Slow Food Revolution*, pp. 167–8.
2. Interview with Serena Milano, co-ordinator of Slow Food Foundation for Biodiversity, who was centrally involved in the development of the International Slow Food Presidia.
3. SF Press Release Terra Madre 2004.
4. Terra Madre speeches: www.slowfood.com
5. A. Capatti, *Slow*, January 2006.
6. Samuel Muhunyu, email communication with author, January 2008.

7. C. Scaffidi, 'Three Realms', *Slow*, January 2006.
8. Ibid.
9. Capatti, *Slow*, January 2006, pp. 8–9.
10. Ibid.
11. Scaffidi, 'Three Realms'.
12. C. Bogliotti, 'The Future of Food', *Slow*, January 2006.
13. C. Petrini, *Buono, pulito e giusto. Principi di una nuova gastronomia* (Einaudi 2005); translated into English as *Slow Food Nation*.
14. Petrini, *Slow Food Nation*, p. 109.
15. Ibid.
16. Ibid., p. 115.
17. Ibid., p. 121.
18. Ibid., p. 135.
19. www.terramadreslowfoodbrasil.com

Chapter 4

1. V. Shiva, 'Celebrating Food Economies', *Resurgence* 229 (2005).
2. Petrini, *Slow Food Nation*, p. 248.
3. P. Freedman (ed.), *Food: The History of Taste* (University of California Press 2007), p. 264.
4. Petrini, *Slow Food Nation*, p. 55. He makes the connection and explains the reason for his update in his document *Taking Back Life: The Earth, the Moon and Abundance*, prepared for the Mexico Congress in 2007.
5. University of Gastronomic Sciences, 2004 Prospectus, p. 8.
6. Slow Food San Diego: www.slowfoodsandiego.org. Interviews with Gordon Smith and Resparata Mazzola.
7. www.chezpanissefoundation.org

Chapter 5

1. W. Berry, 'The Pleasures of Eating', in *What Are People For?* (North Point Press 1990), p. 145.
2. Ibid., p. 146.
3. Ibid., pp. 147, 148, 149.
4. Petrini, *Slow Food Nation*, p. 165.
5. W. Morris, 'The Decorative Arts', Public Lecture, 12 April 1877, in *The Selected Writings of William Morris* (Lawrence and Wishart 1979), p. 51.
6. Ibid., p 67.
7. Ibid., p. 88.
8. Ibid., p. 193.
9. Petrini, *Taking Back Life*.

10. Morris, *Selected Writings*, p. 51.
11. Bogliotti, 'The Future of Food', p. 64.
12. M. Fort, 'Around Britain With a Fork', *Guardian*, 5 January 2008.
13. Petrini, *Slow Food Nation*, p. 172.

Chapter 6

1. Petrini and Padovani, *Slow Food Revolution*, p. 133.
2. B. Anderson, *An Imagined Community* (2nd edn, Verso 1991).
3. Dickie, *Delizia*, pp. 197–9.
4. These figures were announced by Paolo di Croce, Head of Slow Food's international office at the Mexico Congress.
5. According to Slow Food Congress rules this was 1 delegate for every 100 members of countries which had up to 1,000 members: 1 delegate every 150 members between 1,001–4,000 members; 1 delegate every 200 members between 4,001–20,000 members and 1 delegate every 250 members for countries over 20,000 members.
6. This and the following quotations from Petrini are all taken from *Taking Back Life: The Earth, The Moon and Abundance*, Mexico pre-Congress document.
7. See Petrini, *Slow Food Nation*, p. 199 and Bogliotti, 'The Future of Food'.
8. N. Klein, 'Democratizing the Movement', in *Fences and Windows: Dispatches from the Frontline of the Globalization Debate* (Flamingo Harper Collins 2002), pp. 208–9.

Chapter 7

1. D. Massey, *World City* (Polity Press 2007), p. 15.
2. Ibid.
3. M. Montanari, *Food is Culture* (Columbia University Press 2004), p. 139.
4. J. Lymburn, 'The Case For Culinary *Terroir*', *Slow*, April 2005, pp. 62–5.
5. N. Klein, Preface to J. Bosé and F. Dufour, *The World is Not For Sale: Farmers Against Junk Food* (Verso 2001).
6. Ibid.
7. Petrini, *Slow Food: The Case For Taste*, p. 39.
8. Ibid., p. 43.
9. Parkins and Craig, *Slow Living*, p. 100.
10. Berry, *What Are People For?*, p. 113.
11. Ibid., p. 114.
12. Ibid., pp. 114–15.

13. E.F. Schumacher, *Small is Beautiful* (Vintage 1993), pp. 87, 88.
14. Ibid., p. 50.
15. Ibid., p. 57.
16. Ibid., p. 9.
17. J. Akeroyd, *The Historic Countryside of the Saxon Villages of Southern Transylvania* (Fundatia Adept 2006).
18. See for example A. Michaels, 'Not Fast Enough: Why Investing in Italy is Like Driving with the Brake On', *Financial Times*, 22 January 2008.
19. Petrini, *Taking Back Life*.

Chapter 8

1. J. Stiglitz, *Globalisation and its Discontents* (Penguin 2002).
2. J. Gray, *False Dawn* (Granta 2002).
3. J. Stiglitz, interview with Laurie Taylor, *Thinking Allowed*, Radio 4, 28 September 2007.
4. K. Marx and F. Engels, *The Communist Manifesto* (Penguin 1983), p. 83.
5. Petrini, *Slow Food: The Case for Taste*, p. 8.
6. Ibid., p. 26.
7. R. Sassatelli, *Consumer Culture* (Sage 2007), p. 183.
8. J. Stiglitz, *Making Globalization Work* (Allen Lane 2006), p. 285.
9. M. Litvinoff and J. Madeley, *50 Reasons to Buy Fair Trade* (Pluto Press 2007) p. 1.
10. *The World of Presidia* (Slow Food Editore 2004).
11. Petrini, *Slow Food Nation*, p. 52.
12. Slow Food Foundation for Biodiversity, *Social Report* 2006, p. 36.
13. Ibid., p. 30.
14. Petrini, *Slow Food Nation*, p. 198.
15. Stuart Hall in conversation with Bill Schwarz, 'Living With Difference', *Soundings* 37, Winter 2007, pp. 150–1.

Chapter 9

1. Sassatelli, *Consumer Culture*, p. 113.
2. Bourdieu, *Distinction*, p. 7.
3. Ibid., p. 183.
4. These criticisms can be found in detailed discussion in a collection of articles in the journal *Food, Culture and Society*. See J. Labelle, R. Laudon, Janet Chrzan and Marie Sarita Gaytan in Volume 7, Issue 2 (2004), and K. Donati, 'The Pleasure of Diversity in Slow Food's Ethics of Taste', *Food, Culture and Society*, Volume 8, Issue 2 (2005).

5. Ginsborg uses it in his book *Italy and its Discontents* (Allen Lane 2001) in his discussion of new associations and civil society movements.
6. Donati, 'The Pleasures of Diversity', p. 235.
7. J. Rayner, 'Be Honest – Supermarkets Have Made Our Lives Better', *Observer*, 17 February 2008.
8. Z. Williams, 'Jamie's Fowl Sanctimony', *Guardian*, 16 January 2008.
9. N. Perullo, 'Slow Knowledge', *Slow* 57, 2007, pp. 19, 21
10. *Il Dizionario di Slow Food* (Slow Food Editore 2002).
11. Petrini, *Slow Food Nation*, p. 165.
12. J. Rutherford, *After Identity* (Lawrence and Wishart 2007), p. 11.
13. R. Sennett, *The Culture of the New Capitalism* (Yale University Press 2006), p. 4.
14. R. Sennett, *The Craftsman* (Allen Lane 2008), p. 268.
15. Ibid., p 265.

Index